SPECK OF DIRT

by

Thomas E. Kirk

To: Dr. Mays:
Sincerely yours:
Thomas E. Kirk: June 27, 1997

Printed by:
Advocate Press
Franklin Springs, Georgia 30639

Cover photo taken in 1943 shows
Tom Kirk to right of his mom, Vivian.
Sister Nora Jean and Brother Kenneth
are standing in front.

Published by: B. W. Coile Productions,
P.O. Box 224, Comer, Georgia 36029

Library of Congress Catalog Card Number:
93-73503

ISBN 0-9628749-1-4

"SPECK OF DIRT"

All newborn life must bear a gray area of memory and although this time may vary for humans, most of us can remember special events occurring late within the first year. Events prior to this time in a child's life become fact through the information obtained from its mother and her close associates. Recognition of father isn't established until about the second year and prior events will usually go unnoticed. Somewhere between age two and three the child seeks out and accepts its father through instinctive guidance and may select anyone known as father or daddy where affection is noted within the child's immediate family. If no father exists during this sensitive period a child may form a feeling of rejection and try to invent an imaginary father in its mind. This can be most unfortunate and I thank God for my ability to achieve a father's love at my time of transition from the grey area to my first memories of childhood. My Uncle Edwin was born three weeks before I arrived and since he chose my grandfather as his daddy, this meant he was to be mine also. All my uncles and aunts called grandfather, "Daddy" and called my mom "Vivian", so naturally I followed suit. My grandfather was slow to accept me until I began walking and talking, but there was a tremendous amount of love and affection from all members of our large family. A faint memory of tragedy occurred during my second year when life and death came to our home at the same time with the arrival of my Aunt Rachel and the departure of my grandmother. This brought about a closer bond to all those affected and slowly changed the outlook for all the future.

Everyone in the family was required to work all daylight hours in the fields and the babies were tended in shifts. It gave lots of freedom and a good chance for mischief but in a short time the small ones began chipping in to help out. I gathered eggs and helped gather rich pine limbs from the woods. I observed my grandfather and Uncle Horace while they took honey from a bee hive nearby and tested my taster on honey for the first time. The crop of honey grew slim over a short period of time and I knew where some had been hidden. Uncle Edwin helped me to climb the kitchen cabinet in an attempt to get the hidden goods and this cabinet fell over flattening both of us. That failure brought about my first real spanking in memory but I was determined to succeed. I dragged the water bucket to the bee hive and pushed the hive over. When I went inside to get some honey, the bees covered me. I can still smell the anger of those bees and they convinced me then and there, I'd never steal anymore honey. My grandfather raked the bees from my body with his pocket knife and over 100 stingers were removed from my face and head. Some time elapsed with only a faint memory since only a miracle could have saved my life that day and whatever happened was never fully explained to me. I've always liked honey, although I've never tried to test the bees again. I've been exposed to wasp and yellow jackets and they have hit me, but never stung me. Even the mosquito doesn't bother to bite me and this may have been influenced by the amount of bee stings received that day.

I was born in an old house between Colbert and Diamond Hill and shared a short babyhood with the Cruthers and Crumley families. My grandfather Dave worked with constructing the original Highway 29 bridges and my father was known to work with him during a period of this construction. My stays were short lived since grandfather moved about many times and my next stop was a house located between George Christians and Johnny Highlands. Not long afterwards we were living between Shiloh and Pokey near the home of Dan Hinley. It was here that most events began to take shape and people would begin to take more parts in my life and memory. I began helping with the work as required by all in our family and found additional curious playmates in my grandfathers beagles along with the many cats, chickens and farm animals belonging to the family. I helped my Uncle Edwin gather rich pine from the woods and he always insisted on performing the chopping operation. As a result I jerked my pine off the chop block and he cut my right index finger through the knuckle. The finger was held on by the leaders so my grandfather put splints on it, wrapped it with sheet cloth and made me soak it in kerosene for one month before looking at it. The results were amazing and the finger was saved. My fourth birthday arrived here and this was a very eventful year. On that birthday my mom gave me a sunsuit and nick named me "Sonny Boy". Most all the children had nicknames, but little did I know this name would follow me throughout my entire life. Uncle Edwin was "Niggerhead" and Uncle Hoyt was "Con". Others were "Jughead" and "Doutsey" and for the large part I didn't know what our real names were until I grew up. To me, grandfather had become Daddy and I liked to travel with him. It was exciting to carry a wagon load of cotton to the gin near Bond's Store, although this was a long trip and sometimes we would get caught in severe thunderstorms. I would get inside Daddy's raincoat and look out through the slit between button holes. That year Daddy met Blanche McCurdy and got married again. He took me to the wedding in a T-Model Ford and on the way to meet with the Justice of Peace, I sat beside him. However on the way back, Blanche put me over against the door and she sat alongside Daddy. I was annoyed but there wasn't much I could do to change things. Before my fourth birthday my Mom had met a man and shortly after Daddy married, my Mom got married. This just killed me because I didn't like this man. There were many fights and my Daddy and uncles ran the man off several times. We remained living at Daddy's house and on Saturday nights Otha and Anderson Adams would come to play the fiddle and guitar and sing. Sometimes Clustus Tyner would come along and he was really the most fun of all. Anderson later became my uncle when he married my Aunt Ruth and I guess this was to be my first experience of observing courting between the opposite sex.

My brother Kenneth was born late in my fourth year and my stepfather moved us to a tin top house on the road between where Glen Thomas and George Christian were living. We were closer to Shiloh and it also put us closer to my new Granny Leaird's house. I definitely didn't want to go, but my Mom wouldn't let me have my way and my Aunt Jenny gave me a large pine cone to cooperate. This was where I first met Betty Joyce and Martha Jane. Jane was the same age as I and Betty Joyce would dig artichokes for us from our backyard. My stepfather worked with the W.P.A. and was seldom seen, but our mailman Henry Eckels came by every weekday and I enjoyed meeting him for the mail, although he seldom had any for us. I guess he got tired of me pestering him because one day when I ran to the mail box, he stuck out his false teeth and chased me. I thought he had turned into a monster and ran for my life. He later gave me a penny on our front door steps to show he was my friend. Mr. Buck Beard's family were long time true friends of the Kirk family and they never forgot or forsake any of us. They would always visit and share with us, no matter where we moved or who we added to the family. Mitchell Beard was about my age and he would come to play. His favorite game was "Dog, Rabbit and Hunter". It took three to play and many times Martha Jane or Betty Joyce would be the dog. When I hunted Mitchell, I would shoot him by yelling "bang", but many times when I was the rabbit, Mitchell hit me alongside the head with a rock. I often believe he thought I was actually a rabbit when I ran out of the syrup cane field with Martha Jane in hot pursuit. We lived at the tin top house for two years then moved to the Sam Long place in an old haunted house located near John Long's land. This house was in the woods with only a narrow dirt road leading to it. I didn't know what the word "haunted" meant, but while living here I'd get a good education in weird events. My mother and I hand dug a garden around the only fruit tree on the place which was a full grown pear tree. I couldn't cut wood yet, but I could drag rich pine limbs and dead oak limbs to the house for my Mom to cut and burn in the old cast iron cooking stove. In these woods I found an odd nest of chickens. There were two chickens, they were solid white and could swim when placed in the water of a nearby stream. They smelled awful and Mom wouldn't let me bring them home and she insisted I shouldn't play with them. They lived in the bottom of a large hollow tree and after about two weeks they suddenly disappeared. My Uncle Hoyt Adams told me they were young buzzards. We never had any visitors here since it was a far distance to Daddy Kirk's house and the Long family didn't visit anyone. We made a path through the woods to Granny Leairds. This was about three miles and we would walk there on Sunday to have dinner and banana pudding. I made a pig of myself one Sunday eating and I haven't liked banana pudding since then. Shortly after our move to the haunted house, my sister Nora Jean was born and I picked up another unusual task. My job was to get out of bed at 4 a.m. each morning and shake Mom's bed to make Nora Jean stop screaming while Mom fixed my stepfather's breakfast. This went on and on through the winter with little success to quiet Nora Jean, so I started pinching her to make her scream louder, then my Mom would come and get her and hold her in one arm while she was cooking. The house would get deathly quiet when Mom would carry her and I could run back to bed and get my sleep. The house was very cold and all winter I slept with covers over my head. In the spring everything blossomed in beauty. Our garden grew and we had many young pears on our tree, unlike the past year. The only thing enjoyable about the past winter months had been to learn how to hunt opossums with my Uncle Hoyt Adams and Rob Fortson. During the summer that year, I noticed the pears on our tree in the garden had begun to turn yellow. I asked my Mom to allow me to climb the tree and get some but she said they weren't ripe yet. Soon after, we went to Granny Leaird's for Sunday dinner and when we returned the pears were all gone. A strange thing had taken place and my Mom was very puzzled. The ground around this tree was soft garden area and there weren't any tracks or disturbance to the soft soil. None of the limbs or leaves had been touched on this tree and yet what we had seen in the morning was totally different to what we were seeing now. Not long after this happened, I was awakened during the night and could see something moving in our room. Kenneth was asleep alongside me and I lay very still to watch this thing moving along the wall. It was a large grey felt hat and was moving very slowly along the wall about five feet high. I strained my eyes to see someone underneath the hat, but I could see only the wall. Our room had one window and this was covered by a shutter which was open at the time allowing the moonlight to enter the room. The large hat stopped and suddenly came toward me at a rapid speed. I quickly covered my head and waited for the impact. When nothing happened, I began screaming. My Mom came into the room carrying a kerosene lamp and listened to my story. She believed I saw an owl which had entered the room through the open shutter and made me remain in the room. Kenneth went back to sleep, Mom closed the shutter and I lay awake with my head under the cover for the remainder of the night. I wouldn't get out of bed until Mom came for me the next morning. She inspected the entire room for anything unusual, but found nothing. I told Uncle Hoyt Adams about this, but he didn't remark and it was several nights before I could sleep well again and I kept the covers on my head each night. About a month after this incident, my Mom suddenly quieted Kenneth and me in the front room and ordered us to lie on the floor. It was a very dark, foggy night and I watched Mom peek out the window toward the narrow road to our house. She blew out the lamp and sat quietly on the floor with us for a long time. Finally, she made us go to bed but didn't light the lamp. The next morning, I heard her tell my stepfather about seeing someone or something coming along the road toward the house, but it never arrived. A few nights later, I was awakened by a noise in our room. This time the shutter was closed and only a cricket could have gotten inside. I could see the same gray hat faintly moving about our room. This time it was in a different location and looked as if someone was kneeling down and then stood up. I covered my head quickly and quit breathing. My heartbeat sounded like a drum as I pinched Kenneth in an attempt to wake him. Suddenly Kenneth went flying under the bed covers screaming. Then both of us were screaming. My Mom ran into our room with lamp light and pulled the covers away. She took us out of the room and nailed the door shut. We were put on a pallet in Mom's room for the rest of that night. The next day Uncle Hoyt Adams and Rob Fortson came and searched our home. Behind the door to our room they found a large gray hat hanging on a nail, but no one had ever seen this before and many times this door had been closed and this area of the wall was exposed to full view. Mom was washing clothes that morning, so they showed the hat to her and she placed it into the fire under the large black washpot and I watched it burn. Shortly after that day we moved away from the haunted house into an old house by the creek on Mr. Andy Adams land. Here there were many advantages over the past because we had well water, creek water and a cold spring for keeping milk. We had a barn, a chicken house, pig pen and an out house. Most all eyes and ears were on the events of World War II, but the law of the land included mandatory schooling requirements and rumors were, if you didn't go to school you would be put in jail. This prompted putting me in school at Norcross School House near Shiloh. It was a three mile walk or run one-way and I began making this trip daily with Martha Jane. Jane lived about a quarter mile from us and I would meet her to complete the trip to Norcross together. An older boy had started to school about the same time as I and he lived about a half mile further, but followed the same paths and trails to get to Norcross. He was Theron Fortson and lived over near the home of T-Ran Frost. By the time he caught up with me in the mornings, he would already be hungry and would eat both of my biscuits leaving me with no lunch. As a matter of fact, I can't remember a time when Theron wasn't hungry. It didn't take me long to decide on out running Theron to school in order to save my lunch. I would delay him by blowing up paper bags and leaving them in the road. He thought I had dropped my lunch and would search the bags. Later on he would kick the bag to check it without lifting it, so I put a rock inside one and broke his toe. Most every family in Madison County was eligible to get commodity food from the courthouse at Danielsville twice each month and no doubt without these, most of us would have died of starvation. This consisted of flour, fatback, a few fruits and a Baby Ruth candy bar for each child in the family. I have eaten from one candy bar for a week since I knew when it was gone there was no more. Our breakfast consisted of Redeye gravy, fatback and biscuits. Dinner was thickened gravy and bread and many times supper was only bread and jam. When we got our first cow and chickens it was like living in another world because they furnished our milk, eggs and fresh meat. Hunting opossums, rabbits, squirrels and fish wasn't only enjoyable to me, but furnished us with the necessary foods for survival. I was taught all hunting and fishing techniques by old men of the trade and I can never forget them through our wonderful relationships of love and protection. Uncle Hoyt Adams, Mr. Rob Fortson and Mr. Ed Winn were the most leading men of my life and they taught me discipline, honesty and patience.

My first full year at our home on Mr. Andy Adams' land was devoted to hoeing cotton and corn in the spring along with growing sweet potatoes and peanuts. After completing our obligation to hoe the cotton at home, I would accompany Aunt Elvie to hire out on surrounding farms. Aunt Elvie got fifty-cents per day and I got twenty-five cents per day. I never figured this out because Aunt Elvie made me finish a row each time she completed one. During the summer, Kenneth and I made a dam in the small creek near our home. We cut long rectangles of sod from the pasture with an axe and stacked these against rocks and pine logs. Our swimming hole furnished many wonderful memories of recreation and play along with a place of bathing without carrying water to our home. Each time a cloud burst would occur, we labored together to repair or rebuild the dam with more pine logs and sod. In the fall Mom and I picked cotton, shucked corn, pulled peanuts and bedded sweet potatoes. It was the year of my seventh birthday and together, Mom and I picked seven bails of cotton. A bail of cotton consists of around thirteen hundred pounds of raw material. No time was allotted for poking at packsaddles to find their stinger or messing around with grasshoppers. Each time I fell behind on my row I could see Mom turn and look at me from under her bonnet. She reminded me of a highway patrol car with that long switch sticking up from the back pocket of her overalls. I thought of a plan to get out of picking cotton one evening on my way home from school and I cried with a toothache. Late that evening Mr. Rob Fortson arrived to check my tooth. He brought Robbie Sue with him and she watched while he questioned me about which tooth was hurting. Robbie Sue was two years younger than me and she was shy. She hid behind the door as I tried to explain to Mr. Rob that my tooth wasn't hurting anymore, but he insisted that I show him the one which had given trouble. Finally, I put my finger on a perfectly good tooth and said that was the one. Mr. Rob held my mouth open and grabbed the tooth with a pair of pullers. He yanked the tooth out, it fell in the yard and an old hen gobbled it down like a grain of corn and this tooth never, never grew back. You could hear me and Robbie Sue screaming all the way to Mr. Andy Adams' house and I never used an excuse like that again. If I complained with a stomachache, I was given Castor Oil and if I got a cold I got sugar soaked with turpentine, so needless to say I didn't have any stomach pains or colds that became noticeable. That winter I got my first pair of shoes and we got our first pig. My shoes were two sizes too big and turned up in front like a set of snow skis. Uncle Hoyt said I could wear them several winters because my feet would grow to fill them.

Our pig got out of the pen and ran away from home. Mom and I found it over near the creek at Johnny Highland's and chased it back and forth between the creek and our house in the rain until the pig finally gave out and hid in some dead vines covering a rock pile. I used Mom's raincoat to capture the pig by jumping into the vines and wrapping the pig in the raincoat. We repaired the pig pen but it wasn't necessary. That pig had learned a lesson and knew it wouldn't attempt to escape us again. Mom showed me how to remove the first sweet potatoes from their winter bed, explaining to be careful for a snake since they would seek to den with the potatoes to keep warm during the cold winter. Bedding the potatoes had been completed in the fall by making a round mound of dirt, then shape it like a large bowl. It was filled with fresh green pine needles then the potatoes were placed on the needles in a neat cone shape. The cone shape was then covered with a thick layer of green pine needles and dried corn stalks were placed closely around the outside to form a tent. The tent was covered with a thick coating of dirt, leaving a small opening at the top for ventilation. The potato bed looked like an Indian tepee standing in the field with a small pan on top to keep water out. Entry was made on the south side at the bottom by hand. Normally, a burlap bag was used to seal the hole again and recovered with a thick layer of dirt. A crop of potatoes would feed the family throughout the winter by using this method of preservation. Mom and Granny Leaird had canned many vegetables, made lye soap and gathered clay for white wash during the summer and now these tasks all paid off during the winter months, except the white wash. Mom's efforts to white wash our fireplace was all in vain when the winter rains came from the north. The large rock chimney leaked and water blew in from both sides. Many times the fire was completely put out by rain and was impossible to rekindle or restart. Efforts to stop the incoming water by stuffing sacks, papers and mud into the cracks usually always failed. Firewood was plentiful and my stepfather took me into the woods with a cross cut saw. It didn't take long to catch on to sawing, but I was small and could only hold the saw straight for cutting. The hauling and carrying of wood during the winter for heat and cooking was my responsibility and it was a daily scheduled event. If there was no wood, we had no food nor heat and I got a whipping.

Aunt Lou Crumley came to stay with us that winter and she brought the first radio of our lives. It was a wet cell battery powered unit and required a special ground wire. At first all went fine, since I could listen to the Lone Ranger, my stepfather could listen to Walter Winchell, my mother could listen to James and Martha Carson and my Granny Leaird could listen to "One Man's Family". Granny Leaird stayed with us lots of times and she was a very stern and firm person. Normally, she would always give instructions and have her way about things, so Mom and Aunt Lou would steer clear of her and I always made a point to disappear. Aunt Lou was a sharing person and paid no mind to selfish people. She walked with me to Mr. Fitt's general store and bought us a large wash pot. She put a rag through each ear on the pot and we feverishly dragged this pot over the dirt road for two and one half miles to our home. She helped Mom wash our clothes each Saturday and used the wash water to scrub the wooden floors of our home.

In the Spring of 1942, Mr. Rob Fortson gave me my first dog. Her name was Prissy and she acted out her name in a show each time we were together. Uncle Hoyt Adams came by to carry me on my first fishing trip to Mason's Mill and this was unique because he wasn't fishing for bream or catfish. We didn't even carry a pole and worms like sensible fishermen, we carried rich pine splinters and lengths of stove pipe with one end slightly collapsed. Uncle Hoyt and Mr. Rob Fortson carried the pine and stove pipes and I carried a cotton picking sack over my shoulder. Anyone who saw us wouldn't believe we were going fishing, but after walking for about an hour we came to a split where two streams formed the creek that fed the only waters into Mason's Mill Pond. Here we cleared an area for making a small fire and piled rocks around it to make sure the fire was well contained. It was about three miles to the mill from here and although the creek was narrow with overhanging willows and fox grape vines it was shallow in most all areas during this time of year. I was very eager and watched carefully as Uncle Hoyt and Mr. Rob bundled the rich pine. They lit the ends of the bundles in the campfire and instructed me to push my britches legs all the way up to my butt. They only rolled theirs to the knees but I had to go much higher. They stepped into the cold water and led the way. The rich pine torches lit up the creek and surrounding bushes like daylight. They traveled fast through the water and I had to run in water up to my knees to keep up. After traveling about a mile they stopped to rest for a minute, but said they must hurry so the pine wouldn't burn away before we completed our journey. Uncle Hoyt said they would make three trips tonight. Now, I'm not one for questioning something I don't know anything about and normally will wait to watch and learn, but all this hadn't made any sense to me at all. I thought it might be disrespectful to ask, but curiosity was overcoming my respectfulness. I asked Uncle Hoyt to explain what we were doing. He told me every year between the first and fifteenth of April the fish known as mullet would come out of Mason Mill Pond to lay their eggs in the fresh creek water. These fish lay very still on the bottom and can be seen in shallow clear water. The reason we were traveling fast downstream was to stay in the muddy water from our travel path then we would hunt the fish on our return upstream in the clear water. I told him I understood now and we proceeded downstream at a rapid pace for another mile. Uncle Hoyt and Mr. Rob instructed me to watch for snakes because they would follow the light and might strike me if I got too far behind. I tightened my distance from then on and it wasn't long until we reached deeper and deeper water. We stopped here for a few minutes and Uncle Hoyt said this time was to allow the muddy water to flow past us before starting our trip back. When we started back upstream they instructed me to stay close and when they caught a fish they would place it in the cotton sack for me to carry. They began stopping and I could hear them say. "Here"s one". "There's one over there". "Easy, I'll get this one, you get that one", etc. Sure enough, they held the torch high in front of them and gently placed the crushed end of the stove pipe into the water. I could hear the fish flopping inside the pipes and ran back and forth across the creek to receive the fish. I was amazed and by the time we reached the campfire, my sack was half full of fish and I had taken it off my shoulder and had been dragging it through the water for the last mile. Good gracious, I've never had such a wonderful time and when they finished stringing up all those fish, I was ready to do this again. Uncle Hoyt said they always string the fish and hang them on a limb high off the ground so snakes and animals won't get the fish while we make the next trip. The campfire was replenished and this would also keep varmints away. Our trip back downstream and our return the second time was similar to the first and I was ready to go again, but Uncle Hoyt said we had a good haul and we must never be greedy. I was very hungry and asked Uncle Hoyt if these were good to eat. Mr. Rob said that's a good idea so he removed the scales from three fish with his knife. He placed a stick in each and we roasted fish over the campfire. That was the best tasting fish I've ever eaten and I believe that was the most enjoyable fishing trip of my entire life.

Later that year, we got our first cow. I watched through the cracks in the stable while Mom milked our cow each evening and more than once Mom squirted milk in my eyes. My additional assignment was to deliver the milk to the cold spring near the creek and retrieve it to the house each night for supper or at any other time when directed by Mom.

My dog, Prissy, wasn't much of a hunter and could care less about following me to the freshly set rabbit boxes that winter. Uncle Hoyt had a very old redbone hound dog named Queen. She was a hunter from the word go. She readily replaced Prissy in the woods. Prissy always wanted to chase the mailman and would wait a quarter mile away at the mailbox for a chance to chase his car. One morning the inevitable happened and I cried as I buried her near our home. Queen made her trip to our home everyday to see if I could go hunting and she would locate any animal in the woods for me. One of our trips led us to a rock pile in the field and Queen barked constantly at the rocks. She tried desperately to move the rocks with her feet so I began to help. Suddenly, I saw white hair in the rocks and I couldn't hold Queen away from the little animal. Queen had lost all but a few of her teeth through age, but she still grabbed this animal out of the rocks and shook it swiftly about. My nostrils became paralysed from a scent appearing to be all the little pieces of leaves, grass, flowers and wild onions ground up together. I couldn't stop Queen and she tossed the little animal until it couldn't move anymore. Then she ran through the grass, pushing her nose and head into the dirt. I took the pretty little thing by the tail and headed home. When I reached the stream, I could see Mom standing in our backyard screaming at me. I yelled back to tell her and show her the beautiful little animal that Queen and I got. She didn't want any part of us and ordered me to place the little animal on the ground, take off all my clothes, hang them on a limb and get into the stream and start scrubbing with sand. The water was very, very cold, but she insisted I'd never be allowed to come home if I didn't obey. I stayed in the water for a long time before she sent a towel to me by my brother Kenneth and he only came part way, then threw the towel and ran. I got another scrubbing by Mom when I got home, but no one would come near me for a week at school. Later that winter I caught another one of these little beautiful skunks in my rabbit box, but I didn't disturb it. Instead, I returned home and told Mom and that night my step father went to the rabbit box, picked it up and threw it into the creek. Everyone really hated these pretty little animals and didn't mind proving their feelings.

Late in 1944, I became concerned about Mom's silence and grief from the message of Uncle Leonard being missing in action in Germany. About the same time my step-father either lost or quit his job with the W.P.A. and began staying from home and drinking heavily. He began making home brew and teaching me how to watch it work and making me responsible to care for this brew up to and including bottling it. He continued to go on Monday morning of every two weeks to get commodity foods at the courthouse and we still survived with the fish I could catch in my sack seine at the creek. He came home one Monday night to tell of an accident at the Danielsville courthouse building and although no one was seriously hurt, it was still considered bad. The events leading up to the accident were explained to Mom. It so happened that Mr. Clustus Tyner was headed to the courthouse to get his rations and had entered Highway 29 at Bluestone Church on his bicycle which was his sole means of transportation. The bike of Clustus had a large basket on front but didn't have any fenders. Mr. Frost and Mr. Highland had entered the highway just ahead of Clustus and were rolling down the steep hill at a slow pace in their flatbed T-Model Ford truck. Clustus was rapidly overtaking them on his bike but couldn't pass due to a semi-truck coming up the hill from the opposite direction. Clustus didn't have any brakes on his bike and attempted to slow the bike by applying his feet to the rubber of the front tire. The skin burned off his feet and he hit the back of the truck, throwing him onto the truck bed and his bike went into the corn field. Mr Frost and Mr. Highland had been in the woods on Sunday night drinking moonshine liquor and weren't in the best frame of mind. They had a small slit in the back of the truck cab but neither of them would look back to see Clustus. They knew something had landed on the truck and when Clustus began beating on the canvas top, Mr. Highland tried to put his foot through the floor board. They thought a space man had landed on them and tried to evade this creature by driving at maximum speed. Their fright and flight took them straight into the north door of the Danielsville courthouse, leaving the T-Model headlights and fenders plastered to the door seals. Clustus was thrown clear of the truck and casually walked around the scene with all the other spectators. When he got his chance he hit the road running and hitched his way back to his bike in the corn field. Being undamaged, except for the large basket, which he could readily straighten, Clustus proceeded back to the courthouse and picked up his commodities. I always did love Clustus, I'd known him since I could remember and to me, he was my hero, especially after this event.

One problem led to another that year and along with Mom's worry about Uncle Leonard, nothing seemed to turn out right. My stepfather stayed drunk most of the time and started beating Mom every time he came home. Our cat had four beautiful little kittens and they were covered with fleas, so I put them under the wash tub. I sprayed D.D.T. then I sat on the tub for a few minutes. Mom always did this to the house to kill flies. When I removed the tub, all four kittens were dead and if my grief wasn't enough, Mom almost beat me to death with a stick. I've never felt so terrible and I learned a lesson from this, because I thought I could bring them back, but realized then, when you're dead you're gone from here forever.

After several months Mom got word from the government that Uncle Leonard had been captured and was alive. I'll never forget her happiness on this day, but no one else shared this. I was too young to know and there seemed to be no one else around who cared. One of my step-father's drinking buddies had been killed in the war about this time and he was staying drunk and trying to force everyone to grieve about this. Aunt Lou had come back to stay with us for a few months and this wasn't helping our domestic problems. I was getting into more and more problems with my stepfather because I was caught between a rock and a hard spot over the home-brew making disagreement between Mom and my stepfather. My brother Kenneth was still out of the picture and seldom got involved, but I had to be careful not to allow anything to happen to him. We had been poking at frogs in a hole under a large oak tree near the edge of our yard when suddenly we were attacked by several scorpions which got in our clothing before we knew it and one stung Kenneth on the stomach. They got me on the hand and elbow but while Kenneth was screaming, my stepfather lunged at me and swung his fist just short of my face. I always had the instinct to run for my life, but a greater power held me intact to protect my Mom, Kenneth and Nora Jean.

Shortly afterwards, Kenneth and I and our mama cat were chasing rats in our barn loft. A board broke and Kenneth fell to the floor below. I didn't climb down, instead, I jumped out of the loft and grabbed Kenneth in my arms. I struggled to get him to the house and Mom met me. Kenneth wasn't moving and she knew he was hurt badly. His head was cut open and Mom thought he had a fractured skull. Aunt Elvie, Uncle Hoyt and Mr. Rob came and took Kenneth to the hospital at Royston. The doctor sewed his head back together and within a few days he was up and going again. He went with me to Mr. John Long's home twice each week to get fresh clover for our cow and we started stopping by Mr. John's strawberry patch on our return trip. While picking strawberries something bit Kenneth on the hand. His hand swelled bigger than his head, but gradually he showed his toughness and it began to return to normal. I thought I had my problems, but Kenneth could come through the back door and end up between the steps. He got tougher by the day and eventually he could perform side by side with me.

That Christmas we put out our stockings as always and we got the usual orange, apple and candy bar with exception, this year we got some firecrackers. My stepfather got drunk for Christmas and showed us how to light the firecrackers. He burst most of them, but on Christmas day, I found several on the ground with short fuses. They were small, but after applying one of these to a hot wood coal, I realized you don't hold anything with a short fuse. With a numb hand I placed all the others in a small pile and put hot wood coals over the top. After some time I gave up and stirred the pile of coals. An immediate series of bangs erupted and it was all over. About an hour later our home was filling with smoke. Everyone ran outside to find the roof of our porch on fire. No way to get water to the top, we began throwing water through the burning hole from below and sure enough we put the fire out. However, I checked it every thirty minutes for the next two days and continued to throw water on it.

During the fall season that year, we all gathered on our small front porch one night to watch and listen to a terrible storm passing just south of our home. Lightening from this storm completely lit the sky and ground around us and I could hear the thunderous sounds of what seemed to be a long train slowly passing. It moved slowly to the north and eventually went out of hearing but you could still see the huge lighted path of its travel. It was an odd storm since the wind didn't blow at our house and there wasn't any rain. The next day I heard everyone living near us talking about the thing which we had seen and heard. It was call "The Great Tornado" and had cut a one quarter mile wide path along Highway 29 from Mr. Dean's store to Royston. Many people were dead or missing, their homes destroyed and their cows could be seen hanging in twisted mangled trees.

Our school at Norcross had closed for good and all students were being bused to Ila. My walking distance each day was narrowed to one mile and gave me the opportunity to spend more time in the fields. Robbie Sue and Martha Jane caught the same bus and we were still in the same classes at Ila. During the weekends we would gather at Granny Leaird's or at Mr. Andy Adams house for fish fries and sometimes during the winter months the women would cook large opossum dinners. The fish were catfish caught by Uncle Hoyt and myself by trotlines baited with rabbit at Mason's Mill Pond. The opossums were caught during the fall and winter and we kept these in holding pens. They readily adapted to captivity and got real fat on corn bread and milk. I liked the opossum dinners most of all since the meat was delicious and so were the large sweet potatoes which surrounded the opossum during cooking. Bell Adams was our most favored cook for these treats and Mrs. Susie Mae Fortson always made our meals a complete success with beautiful and delicious pies and cakes. A large cast iron dinner bell was located at Mr. Andy Adams home and it rang sharply at noon every day to indicate dinner was ready for men in the field. Only one time did I ever hear this bell ring other than at noon and when this happened Uncle Hoyt stopped his mule and ran over a mile to the house. A young cow had gotten her neck hung in twisted barbed wire and was choking, but Uncle Hoyt quickly cut the wire away and freed her. No one had to tell me to never ring this bell because I realized it was serious business. I started plowing before I could reach the plow handles and would guide the plow by the cross bar. Uncle Hoyt let me use his boy mule but it was too fast for me and since I couldn't keep up I would tilt the plow stock upwards in an attempt to slow the mule by making the plow dig deeper in the ground. This didn't work because the mule would overheat and had to be stopped to avoid collapsing in the hot sun. Mr. Andy told me to use his personal plowing mule because she was very slow and gentle. He hitched her to a harrow early one morning and after harrowing one row of cotton he told me to take over. Mr. Andy always clucked to his mule quietly and said gee or haw at almost a whisper. I took the lines and harrow by the cross bar and clucked to the mule and we proceeded along the row of cotton with greatest of ease. As I went out of sight over the hill, Mr. Andy began his return to the house and we both felt sure this set up would work fine. It did until I reached the end of the first row of cotton and said, "Whoa". The mule stopped, but she turned and looked past her blinders to see me back there. From this point on there would be problems and I guess I knew this by the way the mule had sized me up. She turned around and started the next row of cotton o.k., but only went a short distance then began leading off toward the field of young corn adjoining the patch of cotton. I pulled hard on the right line and yelled "Haw" at her, but she paid me no mind. When she reached the corn field she stopped and began eating the tops from the young corn. I got angry and ran around to the front of the mule and hit her in the mouth with my fist. The wire muzzle cut into my knuckles and I sat down and cried in disgust. After a few minutes, I walked to the edge of the woods and whittled a limb from a thorn bush with the pocket knife that Uncle Hoyt had given me. I returned to the mule, lifted her tail and placed the limb of thorns underneath. She clamped her tail down hard on the thorns and went flying out of the corn field into the woods. I stood there and watched the tree tops shake and listened to the crashing noise as she raced through the thicket of bushes, briers, vines and small trees. When she cleared the other side she was kicking and hee-hawing and carrying on something awful. The only thing left attached to her was that bent muzzle over her mouth and she headed straight for Mr. Andy's house. He was a man of very few words, so I told him what happened before he asked. I'm not sure why, but he didn't offer to let me plow his mule anymore.

Our school at Ila was much better than at Norcross and I enjoyed the recreation facilities, lunchroom and meeting many new friends. There I met Walter Barrett and became good friends. I told him where I lived because he sold Suave salve, a softening salve for the hands and he wanted to sell some to my Mom. On Sunday I watched him come over the hill on his bike and start his decline at a high speed. I yelled to tell him to watch out for the creek, but he couldn't hear me and he hit the water. It was an unusual sight. Walter went flying through the air and he looked like a frog with a hundred cans of salve flying around him. Luckily, he wasn't hurt and we spent an afternoon together after selling Mom two cans of the hand salve. We seined the creek for crawly bottoms and horny heads and got a good catch. Walter loved to fish and shared one of his flips (slingshots) with me to use as a weapon against snakes. He lived up near Mr. Johnny Horne's on the Shiloh/Pokey Road and came often after this first trip.

My stepfather finally found a job with Mr. Rob Beatenbough's sawmill. He got Mr. Rob to hire me on to work weekends as waterboy. I made enough money to buy my first used bicycle. I started attending Sunday School regularly at Shiloh Baptist Church and after begging Mom, she allowed me to attend night services on Sunday. It only took one Sunday night service to convince me that I had no business on the road riding my bike at night. Everything changes after dark and all little bushes and weeds become varmints which move in various directions. Once I made it home that night, I didn't ask to go out alone after dark again.

World War II had ended and Uncle Leonard had been liberated from a German prison camp. Daddy had moved several times within Madison County and had finally landed for a while at Dink's Swamp. Without any transportation we were all still a long way apart, but we beat a path through the woods behind Luther Seymour's store and came out at Mrs. Ruth Fortson's. It was during these trips to Dink's Swamp on weekends that I met Faye Ann. Her mother, Ruth, was a real friend to my Mom and would always give us peas and butterbeans from her garden when we stopped by. On weekends when I didn't show up at Dink's Swamp, some of my uncles and aunts would visit with us. Uncle Hoyt Kirk came one weekend shortly after my stepfather had brought a goat home for us to fatten for killing. The goat had eaten all the grass, weeds, bushes and flowers in our yard and I took it up on the side of our fields to graze. He was a rough goat and would butt you to the ground each time you got near him, so I tied his rope to a bush near the heavy weed growth and there wasn't any way he could have gotten loose. My stepfather came home that Sunday evening drunk and threatened to beat me and ordered me to go get the goat. Uncle Hoyt told him the goat was o.k. where it was and they began fighting. He hit Uncle Hoyt several times with a brush broom and tore his right trouser leg open from his waist to his foot. I threw rocks at him and Uncle Hoyt finally wrestled him to the ground. He yelled for me to bring him some sacks to tie my stepfather up and we would throw him into the creek. My stepfather was too strong for us and he got free. He grabbed my bike and rode off yelling. "I'm going to get a gun and kill all of you". My Mom and Aunt Lou led us through Mr. Andy Adams' pasture and we began running to find someone to help us. Aunt Lou wanted to swear out a warrant for my stepfather and the nearest person representing the law was Mr. Lee Fortson who lived near Shiloh. We traveled through the fields and woods until we reached his home. Mr. Lee wasn't sure about how the law was affected, especially with our long record of domestic problems. We slowly began our return trip home and Uncle Hoyt returned to Dink's Swamp. On our arrival back home, my step father was there and he slapped Mom and Aunt Lou several times. The next day Aunt Lou packed her large blue sack and left on foot to return to her home in Colbert. My Granny Leaird came to stay with us in an attempt to control my stepfather. Mr. Rob Fortson came and talked with him and Mr. Rob told him, "When ever you get the urge to hit someone you come and hit me, don't you let me hear tale of you hitting these women and children again". My stepfather went straight for several months after this event.

Mr. Andy Adams sold his farm and moved to his newly

purchased land and home up on the main road to Ila. Uncle Hoyt Adams began building him a house up there and moved away shortly afterward. Mr. Dewitt Adams moved his family over near Dink's Swamp taking Martha Jane and Betty Joyce and Mr. Rob Fortson moved his family to a house near where Mr. Andy lived taking Robbie Sue and Peggy with him. This not only left Nora Jean, Kenneth and myself with no one to play with, it also removed our family security and the school bus couldn't make the trip down there just to pick up two students. Kenneth and I were out of school for several weeks until my stepfather found us a vacant house on the Ila road between the homes of Mr. Albert Carey and Mr. John Horne. This move caused several more weeks delay in schooling for me and I was set back one year. Martha Jane started her school in Danielsville and Robbie Sue jumped one year ahead of me at Ila. Finally, things began sorting themselves out in my mind and I became more receptive to my future. I graduated from grammar to high and came into a different environment with different teachers and different friends. My most respected teacher was Mrs. Clara Tyner because I could comprehend her assignments and I learned a lot during her classes. My most admired teacher was Mrs. Jackson because she was a beautiful queen in my eyes and I enjoyed her nearness to me. My most dreaded classes were with Mrs. Birdie Freeman because she wasn't only stern and firm, she would put a beating on you first and find out your name later. All my teachers meant business however they went about it differently. Andrew Adams sat directly in front of me in Mrs. Freeman's class and although Andrew was my good friend, he put me in some real hot spots at times. I got the buttons jerked off my shirt many times because of Andrew and many times I didn't know the cause. Mrs. Freeman was constantly watching Andrew because he chewed tobacco in class, but Mrs. Freeman never proved this. Many times during study period, she would come sneaking up to his desk from behind, grab him and pry his mouth open to find nothing. Andrew could eat Brown's Mule Chewing tobacco as easy as he chewed it and Mrs. Freeman never understood this. Most all the students didn't mind when Mrs. Freeman swung the paddle at them for doing wrong because they knew Andrew had already slit the paddle with his knife, so all they had to do was put up their elbow and the paddle would fly apart on contact. Mrs. Freeman never hit me with a paddle, but she would shake me until the buttons flew off my shirt and Andrew would laugh until he cried to see this. Once he broke wind loudly in class during study period. He turned around and looked at me real hard. All the other students looked at me and Mrs. Freeman jerked all the buttons off my shirt. Another time he shot Mrs. Freeman on the open portion of her breast with a spit ball, then flipped the rubber band on the floor by my desk, turned and looked at me as if I was crazy. When Mrs. Freeman grabbed me that time the spit ball was still stuck to her chest and she shook me until my britches almost fell off. What Andrew didn't know was, each evening when I arrived home with buttons missing from my shirt, my Mom gave me another beating for lying to her. It all came to a head that winter when Andrew tackled my friend Tommy Brown outside the ball field during a friendly game of football. Tommy wasn't only outside the ball field, he was in the highway running for his life from Andrew. I objected and Andrew filled my ball cap full of snow and stomped it into the muddy field. I challenged Andrew to a boxing match and the school principal not only allowed it, but encouraged it. Andrew had a one foot height advantage and a one foot reach advantage on me, but I didn't believe he could really hurt me. If I had been thinking clearly, I could have beat him severely around the knee caps, but I went after him like I knew what I was doing. The big gloves which the principal furnished were very heavy and clumsy and we flailed at each other like spiders. Suddenly Andrew hit my glove and turned my thumb all the way back facing me. I yelled and turned around to remove the glove and Andrew hit me in the back of the head and sent me plowing into the dirt. I jumped up mad and lunged at Andrew landing straddle his waist facing his back side. I beat and kicked until the principal broke up our boxing match. From that day on Andrew stood by my side through any event and he has always been one of my best friends. During my initiation to the Future Farmers of America (FFA) Andrew encouraged me and gave me my first chew of Brown's Mule tobacco just before I was to enter the high school basement. We were blindfolded and led through the basement door individually, so no one left outside knew what he had coming. I was wallowing this chunk of tobacco around in my mouth when a man came out the basement door and told me to remove my shoes, socks and roll my britches legs up. He put a dark blindfold over my eyes and led me through the door. I thought we might wade through water or mud inside, but instead, I was left standing on a cold piece of metal sheet. I heard a squelching sound and suddenly felt a tremendous electrical current paralysing my body. I jumped high in the air only to land on this thing again. My next move was to run off the metal sheet and of course this was the name of the game. It was over as quickly as it started, but the chunk of tobacco was gone and I hadn't spit it out. I was green and sick for two days afterwards and I never touched chewing tobacco again.

Our home was three months behind in rent and Mr. John Horne offered a resolution to the problem by letting us farm several acres of his land on halves. I sold my bike and caught a ride to Danielsville to talk with a man who had a mule, wagon and the entire lot for $15.00 and I drove the mule, pulling the wagon and farm equipment back to our home. I plowed the land on weekends and after school each evening to produce a crop of cotton in an effort to buy food and pay our rent. On moon lit nights, I would plow the field until I couldn't see anymore. I began missing more and more days at school and other than my Mom, no one really cared whether I got an education or not. I went to school as often as the farm work load permitted, but this would prove not to be effective. Mr. Ed Dean drove our bus and stopped daily to pick us up. But he barely knew what I was doing on his bus. He didn't like me because I wasn't a steady student and when someone threw Kenneth's cap out the bus window near Mr. Bob Langford's, he didn't recognize me asking him to stop the bus. He finally stopped the bus, but when I went running back to get the cap, he drove off and I walked three miles home that day. Needless to say, I informed Kenneth that if his cap went out the window again he would be the one to retrieve it.

My step father continued working at the sawmill, but gambled his money and this increased the burden on me of making sure the farm produced. He didn't come home until Sunday night and was always drunk and beat my Mom for complaining of no food or responsibility. I got us through the first year and paid off our rent to Mr. John Horne. I made up my mind this type of life must stop. I traded my mule and wagon for a 22 caliber rifle and two cartridges. It wasn't my plan but during the next few days, I killed two squirrels with the only shells I had. On Sunday night, when my stepfather arrived drunk and started beating my Mom, I climbed the side of our rock chimney and took the rifle from where it had been hidden. Nora Jean slept with Mom in our living room and Kenneth slept with me in our only bedroom. Kenneth got up and asked me what I was going to do and I told him I would stop this now and forever. There was a curtain separating the doorway to each room and Kenneth followed me as I pushed the curtain aside. The large room where Mom and Nora Jean slept had a wood heater rigged from the original fireplace and a heater pipe reached out about ten feet into this room. The heater pipe was about six feet off the floor and you could readily walk underneath. When I stepped through the curtain I placed the unloaded rifle to my shoulder and aimed it at my stepfather's head. I yelled out, "Stop this, you leave this home now, you are not needed here and you are not wanted here." My Mom ran to me, pulling at the gun and screaming, "No, no, he's not worth any portion of your life, don't shoot him, please, please, give me the gun!" My step-father was startled and placed his hands on the back of a wooden chair. He pleaded for me to give him the gun, but all the time he was pushing the chair and creeping closer to me.

Suddenly, he raised the chair swiftly over his head and threw it at me. The chair hit the heater pipe and all this pipe came tumbling down rendering the entire room full of smoke and soot. I threw the gun toward where I though he might be an ran out the front door with my Mom, Nora Jean and Kenneth. I ran two miles and came to the home of Mr. Barrett. I asked him to adopt me or let me live in his home, but he refused and took me back to locate my Mom in his 34 Ford. When we arrived at my home, my step father was out in the front yard. He had broken the stock off the rifle and was waving the barrel as a weapon. Mr. Barrett tried to enter the property to search for my Mom, Nora Jean and Kenneth. He made me remain in his car and I saw him knock my stepfather to the ground with his fist. He returned to the car and told me my Mom and the kids are gone, but where do you want me to take you? I knew my Uncle Chandler and Aunt Rounette would welcome me if I was in trouble, so he took me to their home near Mr. Buck Beards. They welcomed me and took good care of me and Uncle Chandler went looking for Mom, Nora Jean and Kenneth. He found them at the home of Mr. Bennett Adams and took them to the home of Daddy, who had now moved to Madison Springs.

My schooling was again seriously disrupted and it seemed nothing could go right. Uncle Chandler rented and farmed land owned by Mr. Buck Beard and immediately put me in the field picking cotton. To ease my mind he told me my Mom and the kids were safe at Madison Springs with Daddy and he was going back to get our things from the house. He would get my clothes and Uncle Horace would help him haul the furniture. On my first day in the field picking cotton, a beautiful young woman brought me water and unbeknowing to me this was Pauline. She set off the same feelings in me which I had received from my teacher at Ila, Mrs. Jackson. I wasn't sure what was happening to me because my Mom had always been very strict about my movements and this curtailed my thinking to a great extent. As it turned out Pauline and her family became some of my most cherished friends in life and I never found out what I was really thinking about that day. Shortly afterwards, Uncle Chandler moved down near North Broad River near Mr. Ben Beard and I helped him set up farming in the bottoms along with helping Harold Beard at his syrup mill. It was here with Uncle Chandler when I broke all records of catching rabbits. I caught thirty-one rabbits one day in thirty-one rabbit boxes and sold them dressed for thirty-one cents each. I loved living with Uncle Chandler and he was a great person in my environment, but I worried about Mom and the kids. My cousin Pete was born and it wasn't long before I was keeping him at home while my Uncle Chandler and Aunt Rounette were at the movies in Athens.

The bus to Ila wasn't available from Uncle Chandler's

and he tried to keep me in school by carrying me to Ila and picking me up in his 1934 Ford. The gas gauge on Uncle Chandler's car didn't work so he would put one gallon of gas in and use it until it ran out. We would then walk to the nearest station and get another gallon of gas, usually on credit. By using this technique, I walked more miles than I rode, until one evening, we tried to crank the car after putting in gas and it wouldn't start. Uncle Chandler said we would pour some gas in the carburetor and when he hit the starter the engine caught on fire. Uncle Chandler slapped his hat over the carburetor and it burned that also, so he yelled at me to help him put dirt on the fire. I threw dirt into the carburetor and we never were able to crank the car again. I couldn't get to school again and dropped back another grade at Ila. Uncle Chandler decided to put me into school at Danielsville High, because that bus came nearby. He borrowed Harold Beard's truck and carried me to Ila to get my school records for delivery to Danielsville. The principal at Ila didn't have any method of transferring my records so he sealed them in a large brown envelope and told me to deliver them to the principal at Danielsville, As we headed toward Danielsville, Uncle Chandler asked me if I had ever seen my school records. I told him no and we stopped and went through them. My grades weren't bad, but my absentee record was terrible. A letter from the Ila principal had also been inserted, alerting Danielsville High to watch out because I was a serious problem child. Uncle Chandler said, "do you know what to do with this letter"? I indicated no. He said, "You can either tear it up and throw it out the window or you can eat the results later." Not knowing what he really meant, I tore it up and threw it out the window.

About this same time my Mom moved out from Daddy's house at Madison Springs and rented a house from Mr. Zeb Dean. I moved back with her to support our family and my schooling ended again. I was approaching my acceptance to the ninth grade, but I would never make it. I hired on with Mr. Zeb to serve gas at his station and also cut pulpwood during the week with Uncle Grover. We worked from sun up until sundown, Monday through Friday and handled the complete operation of cutting the trees, sectioning them in five foot lengths, stacking, loading, hauling to Comer and loading the wood onto open flat rail cars. My gloves wore through fast and pine resin would sometimes build up on my palms to be one half inch thick. During the weekends my work was much easier at Mr. Zeb's store and consisted mostly of servicing and gassing up cars. Mr Zeb would play "Down Yonder" on the juke box and jitter bug for hours to this music. When the pulpwood business died out, I applied for work at Royston Ford Co. and hired on as a body finishing helper. It was here that I bought my first used car on credit and used it only for going to and from my job. It had mechanical brakes and most of the time it didn't have any brakes at all. The right rear fender fell off and I drove it without a fender, since the tail light was on the left fender. Mom got her a job at the sewing plant in Royston and decided to give my stepfather another chance. She moved to Royston taking Kenneth and Nora Jean out of school at Dainelsville and restarting them at Royston. I went to live with Daddy at Madison Springs and worked with all my uncles and aunts on the farm until June 1950. I got Uncle Chandler to drive me to Athens and I visited the Navy recruiter. A few days later I was on a pullman train headed north to Great Lakes, Illinois leaving all my friends and loved ones behind. I know we never had much in life, but we had love and we shared togetherness. When I go back and look now, I find nothing there to reflect these wonderful memories and so many of these beautiful relationships have passed through the pearly gates and are at rest in peace. Practically every home where I once lived are undergrowth and trees. Mason's Mill Pond and all my favorite fishing holes are gone forever, leaving only the golden memories of a few who knew and recognized the value of those most wonderful days in our lives. Even the animals have changed and seem frustrated and afraid as life among us all is allowed to dwindle and take on no fruitful meaning, inevitable to become just another speck of dirt.

"SNIPE HUNT"

Almost from the beginning of life, a child seeks ways of awareness through exploration and by observation of its parents and their friends. Some become exposed to violence while others receive loving care. However, all of them are subjected to respect of their elders in one way or another.

Mine developed around older men, of whom I admired as I grew and "Yes sir" or "No sir" became a part of my everyday speaking in life. I think one of the more realistic ways to express this respect would be to tell you about a true man to boy experience of which I could never forget. However, I was looking at it from a child's view and later tried this on a man of my same age just to observe the adverse results.

It all started on the bank of a small lake in Madison County, Georgia. On a bright sunny, Sunday afternoon I was sitting on a log along side Mr. Ed Winn as we attempted to catch some bream. Uncle Hoyt Adams and Mr. Rob Fortson were at other spots around the lake trying their luck. Mr. Ed shook constantly from some sort of nervous condition, but he was a wonderful old man and I admired his courage and effort. He would always challenge the activities of any man and achieved every job I've ever seen him set out to do. Today he was bound and determined to get that bream, which was nibbling at the worm on his hook. The bobber would only move slightly and the fish couldn't have been as big as the worm, but he was set to jerk that fish's head clean off. I watched his deep concentration and also observed a fly, which Uncle Hoyt called a "cow fly" circling around his head. I always thought they looked more like a miniature horse fly with white stripes on its belly and I knew better than to let one light on me, because his bite would send you sailing into the lake.

Suddenly, the fly lit on Mr. Ed's receding forehead and before I could get any words out of my mouth, Mr. Ed dropped his fishing pole and left his entire hand print embedded into his face, nose and forehead. At that instant, a bird flew from the waters edge almost under my foot and it made a loud, swift, fluttering sound as it flew rapidly across the pond. No one got a real good look at it and I thought it was a quail. I wondered how a bird could have sat there at my feet for so long and be so quiet without me seeing it. Not far away, Uncle Hoyt had heard the slap which Mr. Ed gave himself and the bird fluttering across the pond, so he yelled to Mr. Rob, saying he had heard a snipe. They began calling to each other, how wonderful it would be to catch some snipes while the birds were in this part of the country and my ears were really perked up, catching every word. When they approached us, still talking about snipe hunting, Mr. Ed told me not to giggle at him or tell them about the fly or he would pop me. Their questions about the hand print on his face went unanswered, but as we headed for home I had a lot of unanswered questions to ask about more interesting things. They ranged from, "when are we going snipe hunting", "oh, boy can I hold the sack?"

My Aunt Elvie spent the entire week sewing cotton seed sacks together and I spent my time checking on her progress. I had described these large birds to my mother, how good they were to eat and Uncle Hoyt had said it should be easy to catch a large sack full. She paid me little attention, because I was always dreaming or telling her of big catches.

Saturday night finally came and we left to catch these snipes, with everyone at home acting like it was just another routine opossum hunt. I thought to myself, "I'm gonna show you all something when I get back this time". Uncle Hoyt and Mr. Rob walked through the woods and swamp ahead of me looking for a good location with the one and only lantern we had. Mr. Ed didn't come that night and I found out later, he hadn't approved of this hunt in the first place.

It was a very dark, still night and Uncle Hoyt said it was an ideal night to hunt the snipe, because they wouldn't be able to see the sack seine which I would be holding.

We had been walking almost three hours through thick underbrush and swamp when Uncle Hoyt found the very ditch we had been looking for. We placed the sack seine across a narrow place in the ditch and put rocks on the bottom to hold it down. Uncle Hoyt tied one end to a snag and told me to hold the other end. According to his instructions, he and Rob would walk up and around the ditch, then enter the ditch and scare up the birds on their way back. He said the birds would fly in a large, closely packed covey and would stay low in the bottom of the ditch. If I should make any moves, it would scare the birds away. I was to remain totally still. When the birds hit the back of the sack seine, I was to jump across to the other side of the ditch, trapping the birds inside. They asked if I felt o.k. and then left with the lantern. I watched them disappear through the bushes and realized it was darker down here than I had figured. However, I braced myself and got a good posture ready to receive two or three hundred of these big birds. I began thinking of how proud my mother would be of me, because we would have enough birds to eat on for maybe two months after Uncle Hoyt and Mr. Rob divided up my share. Well, at least we would have plenty until I could come back and get another batch. I thought of how mad Mr. Ed would be when he heard of our big haul, but I'd make him happy by giving him some of my share and ask him to come with me on another hunt right away. We could even come back during the week while Uncle Hoyt and Mr. Rob were working. I was sure I could remember the way and if we got all of them out of this ditch tonight, I knew of other spots which should be equally as good. My thoughts drifted back to the very spot where I stood and it seemed that time was passing very slow and it was very dark. It was kinda like sitting near a large oak tree while opossum hunting with Uncle Hoyt at night and waiting for old Queen to open up on a fresh track, but during those times we always had the lantern by our side. Some of those nights I had been very tired from plowing ground or picking cotton all day and would actually take a nap against the tree, surrounded by the confident security of Uncle Hoyt. The thought crossed my mind that Uncle Hoyt and Mr. Rob may have got lost, but I shrugged it off because Uncle Hoyt knew these woods like the back of his hand. By now, I had lost track of time and there were little noises beginning to break the dark silence around me. I braced myself, without moving, thinking possibly this could be an indication that the birds were coming. To my disappointment the next noise I heard was behind me and not coming from the direction in which I was looking. I stared straight ahead and froze in my britches. I figured whatever was back there wouldn't see me if I didn't move. So I took long, slow breaths to avoid making my body expand. Maybe it would think I was a tree and pass on by, then on second thought, maybe it's a tree climber and begin climbing up my leg. I was rapidly searching my brain for which was more important, the birds or my safety. For some reason the thought of taking home a bunch of snipes was no longer a priority. Suddenly, I saw something move ahead of me but then didn't see it. I did see something and the more I thought of it, the more I was convinced something was lurking there. The chill bumps completely covered my body and seemed to be crawling on my skin. My lips were trembling along with my legs starting to go numb and my eyes were searching frantically to see through the darkness. I could feel other eyes staring at me, but I couldn't see them. Tears began dropping off my cheek and I knew I was fixing to break, but also knew when I did there would be no stopping me and no turning back. I realize now I didn't have the slightest idea of where I was nor did I know which way to go. However, the time had come when I no longer had personal control over my body and unconsciously my brain had taken possession of my soul. Suddenly, I sprang from the ditch and was tearing my way through bushes, trees, honeysuckle vines, bamboo briars and swamp canes. I ran, I fell down, I ran for my life. There may be something back there coming after me but its not going to be easy to catch this boy tonight. I was barely getting my senses back in place when I shot out of the woods into an open field. I kept to the field because the briars and limbs had almost ripped all my clothes off and my body was aching with cuts. The field led me to a dirt road and for the first time I could see where I was running. There was a white soil on the road and this made it light up in the darkness, also it made me believe a school bus would travel this road, so maybe there would be a house with people to tell me the way to my home. Suddenly, out of the darkness on my right, was a house and as I ran toward it, I realized it was where Mr. Rob lived. I now knew where I was and how to get home so I didn't break stride. I passed Uncle Hoyt's house, then shot past where Mr. Andy Adams lived like a bullet. I heard old Queen and the other dogs run out barking but I didn't have any time to stop and say hello. My mother let me in and practically bathed me in rubbing alcohol which was much worse than the beating I had received while running through the woods.

My mom was terribly mad and left early the next morning to go bless out Aunt Elvie and Uncle Hoyt. Aunt Elvie said Uncle Hoyt had returned to the house during the night to get his dog call horn and Mr. Rob had gone with him to hunt me. They had been gone all night and we should go hunt for them, however, they come back and everyone started yelling at each other. All the old folks stayed mad with each other for a long time, but I got over my hurt and never felt hard toward anyone. I know Uncle Hoyt and Mr. Rob came back down that ditch, maybe not in pursuit of birds, but at least they came back for me.

Nineteen years later, while attending Metallurgical Engineering School at San Diego, California, I made friends with a man from Arizona and he mentioned a similar experience. During class break one day, we were approached by a young engineer from the Bronx in Brooklyn, New York. It was obvious he had never been exposed to the country and knew little if anything about animals and birds of the wild. It seemed to be the ideal opportunity to see if a snipe hunt would work as good for us as it had with us. We told the young man about the wonderful times we had catching the snipes and since the method was simple, he was ready to get started. We let him sleep on the idea and built his enthusiasm until the weekend. During this time, he placed a call to his mother in Brooklyn and she sent him $50.00 through Western Union to let him support the trip. He told us his mother was very happy that he had met a couple of nice southern boys who took an interest in making his stay out there so enjoyable. To say the least, this almost foiled our plans, but we were in too deep by now and had no way of backing out. The young man bought a tank of gas for my friends car and three cases of Fallstaff beer. On our way out of San Diego on Saturday afternoon, we stopped at a Quik-Mart and he bought a cooler, 10 pounds of ice, and a sack of apples. About 20 miles east of San Diego, we took a road into the desert. As we passed through the valleys, I could see adobe huts of mud on the steep hillside and began having second thoughts again about this trip. I knew my buddy from Arizona was thinking the same, but by now we were both afraid to make any admission. About 5 miles from the highway, we came across a spot and the gully looked like a good place for the birds to roost over night. We waited at a distance and drank a cold beer until dark. My buddy drove the car back over the hill and came back to help set the trap. We set up one single large sack with rocks on the bottom and instructed the young man to fall across the front when the birds flew in. I went back to the car and got him two cold beers and two apples from the bag and gave them to him before starting up the ditch. It had gotten pitch black except for starlight and after only traveling a short distance, we cut around the hill to the car. My buddy let the car roll to the bottom of the hill and started it in gear so as to make sure the young man didn't hear the motor. When we returned to the camp on Sunday night, we slept in the car while hidden outside of camp. The young man didn't show up at school on Monday and the school administrator sent for me and my buddy. He told us he had spent most of Sunday calming the young man down and if we didn't go with him to the man's room and apologize for what we had done, he would suspend us. We did what we were told and after the apologies our administrator asked the young man what we could do to repay him. He said he had torn his trousers and had to pay for a cab from the other side of San Diego. He had also lost the remainder of the money his mother had sent him and we drank up or ate up the rest. He told the administrator his cost for the snipe hunt was about $200.00. The following pay day, we each gave him $100.00 and he began laughing. Then he gave us back $75.00 each and said he had one of the most wonderful times along with learning a very valuable lesson that night. Another thing he said, "you can both eat your hearts out, because you will never know what actually happened to me out there in the dark desert that night".

"SAWMILL"

My first job of any real responsibility was as a part time waterboy for Mr. Rob Beatenbough's sawmill. It was a real challenge to me and offered an opportunity to make my own money to buy things I wanted and to start a savings of my very own. I went to school five days each week and worked at the sawmill on Saturdays. I was picked up by a labor truck at 4 a.m. and returned at 8 p.m.. My stepfather worked at the same mill and it was through his recommendation that I got the job.

There were several advantages to having a job which paid real money in Madison County and some of these I would soon experience. The sawmill was always located near the creek or river and finding a fresh water spring posed no problem. However, the men always started cutting trees at the mills location and worked their way outward. After a few weeks of operation, yells for waterboy could be heard two miles from the mill in three directions near a river and four directions when located near a creek. When night came each Saturday I always thought only of my good warm bed. I would cover my route going from man to man as rapidly as possible so I could return to the area where the tractors hooked logs and pulled them over the hill toward the mill. The big Farmall didn't offer much excitement but the little Ford would get up on its back wheels and zig-zag over the hill. One of the men told me that was called "walking". Some times when I came to the mill hands, Mr. Rob would stop pulling on that big handle which guided the log through the saw and take a drink of my water. We normally drank from a gourd at home, but Mr. Rob made me use a large porcelain coated green dipper. The large metal bucket held two gallons and sometimes I'd have to drag it because of my height and exhaustion. All the men watched out for me and always seemed to know where I was when a tree was falling.

When it came a thunderstorm the woodsmen always returned to the mill and normally it would rain hard for hours at a time. Mr. Rob would shut down the mill and everyone would load into the labor trucks. They would drive to an old abandoned wood house and commence to play poker, using matches for money. Some men would lose as much as a months wages in one afternoon. They took me along with them once when I had first begun working at the mill, but I didn't enjoy this so I was left behind from then on. During my one and only trip, I explored the old house while they played their games and I found this place ready to fall. The loft was very unsafe and had a couple bundles of hay up there. Most all the windows had rotted out and the doors had long fallen off. There were several storms in the afternoon during that first summer and most evenings the truck wouldn't pick me up until after dark and several times I was beginning to think they had forgotten me. Everyone always seemed happy and I couldn't tell who won or lost that day. Then one afternoon, everyone except myself had gone to the old house at the beginning of a storm. As soon as the rain slacked off, I left the lumber shed and walked through the bull pen to the top of the huge pile of slabs. I wondered how a man could hold out to carry large slabs up this pile then return for another, and another from before sun up till dark everyday. I walked to the top of the pile and I could see over the trees and was watching the fog rise around the tree tops when suddenly, I heard an explosion. It came from toward the old house and I could see smoke and dust rising up like a large cloud coming out of the ground. I could see the tops of bushes shaking and tree tops moving. The entire woods had come alive with men running for their lives. I ran off the slab pile and among some of the men arriving, eager to find out what happened. Most of the things I heard them say they figured had happened, can't be written in this story, along with lots of things they were saying in general. Some of the men had ripped their clothing and most all of them were covered with trash and dust. When Mr. Rob arrived he told everybody to get quiet and help him check to see if anyone was missing. You wouldn't think men in a situation like this would have been so concerned about a small boy, but they must have called for me a dozen times. I tried to tell them I wasn't even there in the first place, but there was a lot of confusion. Mr. Rob said someone had tried to kill all of us and he was going to get to the bottom of this. We all loaded into the trucks and drove by the remains of the old house, as we left for home early. As we passed slowly I could see the roof and loft had caved in completely and one side had fallen flat to the ground. There was smoke and dust still rising up but no fire and there was some holes in the remaining walls which looked like the men had run through them in the panic. Mr. Rob or no one else ever solved the mystery. It was believed to be dynamite since the owner was a religious man, however I always believed it was struck by lightening.

I continued working each Saturday, but when it rained Mr. Rob would send everyone home and dock our pay, unlike when the men had a gambling place. By now I had built a different social environment around me and had new friends which knew I was working for cash money. What they didn't know was my mother had to use most of it to buy food and clothes for the family and I got the small amount when there were leftovers. I had met Clarlyne Long on the bus to school and she had told me I could sit with her if I would do something with my hair. So when I got ready for bed each night I would put several of my mom's large hair clamps on my head. Before long I had waves which would put the English Channel to shame and this was acceptable to Clarlyne so I was happy. Shortly afterwards, I bought me a used bike and polished it 50 times on the first day. This was my pride and joy, not to mention the fact it was the only means of transportation in the family. Going to Marvin Fortson's store and to church at Shiloh on Sunday was no problem now and I put a lot of miles on this bike in a short time. By now Clarlyne had gotten braver and told me if I came to prayer meeting on Sunday night I could sit with her and her father and mother. I readily accepted but ran into a problem on Sunday evening when I asked my mother to let me go to church that night. She said my stepfather had been gone since Saturday morning and she wanted me to stay at home. I begged and finally she gave in, but only if I rode with Mr. John Long and his wife in their buggy. She said I could ride my bike to the mailbox and hide it in the bushes, but I wasn't to ride the bike to church, because I didn't have any lights. I put on the best pair of overalls I had and went to the mailbox and waited for Mr. John. When he arrived, he was late and was trotting his mule as she scooted along the dirt road towing their buggy. I waved at him and he waved back, but didn't stop so I fell in behind on my bike. It was then when I noticed he had a lantern mounted on back of the buggy and it dawned on me that I would have no problem following his light at night so I passed him up and sped off to Marvin's store. I needed to put some air in my tires and felt sure my mother would understand. After I put air in the tires and ate a chocolate covered ice cream called a "honkey", I went to church. I was early and so was Mitchell Beard and he rode his bike also. We got into a race and I beat him for a nickel which I put in the offering cup during prayer meeting. There weren't many people at church however, Mr. John's son Johnny and his new wife were there along with Clarlyne, her mom and pop and Mr. and Mrs. Lee Fortson. Most of the others I didn't know so I sat next to Clarlyne and Mitchell sat by me. After services broke and everyone had gone, I waited patiently outside for Mr. John and his wife to leave. After a while I grew impatient so I entered the church and asked Mr. John when he was going down the road. He cleared his throat and said, "we're not going back home tonight, sonny, we're spending the night with Johnny". I turned and as I left I thought, "oh my God, I'm in trouble". I knew I couldn't stay in the church because they would lock it up for a week, I'd starve to death, and anyway, I had to go to school tomorrow morning. One thing for sure, I wasn't going to stay in that graveyard. I realized no one around there knew me well enough to put me up for a night and the best thing to do was get up enough courage to make it home and not do this again. After I got outside the church lights, my eyes began adapting to the darkness and I could see the road well enough to move along slowly. About one half mile from the church, I turned right onto the road which wound around curves and was mostly all downhill travel to where I lived on the creek. The county had hauled in a gray white soil and packed it on the narrow road so the school bus wouldn't get stuck in red mud. The soil reflected light from the stars and I could readily distinguish the road from the ditch on each side. The farther I went the faster I moved and the small bushes along side the road seemed to move in and out, as if they were some sort of animal. I came over a small rise then dropped down a steep hill and was about two miles from home when suddenly, and in a split second, I saw a large black object and went crashing into it. I was flying through the air like a frog. I hit the road bank and went sliding into a corn field half buried in the soft dirt as my body plowed a deep furrow into the ground. By the time I came to a stop I was already on my feet and running in mid-air. I ran right over the top of my bike, which had bounced end over end for about fifty feet down the road. I grabbed it up, still running for my life and made the wheels over take me. I could hear the thing which I had hit tearing all the corn stalks down back behind me, but I couldn't tell which way it was going. I finally made it onto my bike and set back on the pedals for all I was worth. Then I discovered the handle bars were turned halfway around and were facing the wrong way, but there was no time for making adjustments right now. I knew I had hit a huge black bear and he wouldn't be far behind me.

My mother was still up and I could see the faint lamp light in the window of the house before my heart ever started beating correctly. I ran the bike under the house and threw myself upon the porch. The door flew open and I fell into the room screaming and pointing behind me. My mom slammed the door shut and turned all the cross latches to keep whatever was after me on the outside. Then she grabbed me and tried to calm me down, holding me while the fright poured from my body into a mumbling, jumbled up story, which I had no idea where to begin telling. Later, I washed and went to bed, still sniffling and breaking into a cold sweat.

Almost an hour later, someone came stomping onto the porch and began banging on the door. My mother called out and it was my stepfather. When she opened the door I could see him from my bed. He wore sandals and one was missing, his big toe nail was almost torn off, his britches leg was ripped open all the way to his waist and he had pine needles all over him. He was yelling about a brahma bull which butted him down into the ground up there on the road when he came out of the cornfield. He said that bull kept coming back and butting him down, maybe five times. He was ruptured at a young age and had to wear a truss. He said the truss had kept the bull from goring him to death. He was going up the next day and back track this mean bull and sue its owner.

My mother told him, "I keep telling you something bad is going to happen to you if you don't quit hanging out every week-end over there drinking and gambling these kids food and shoe money away". He was very quiet now, so she came in my room, patted me on top of the head and placed the covers around me.

I never told anyone about this happening and I'm sure my mother didn't either. Later I was asked by some older boys, if I knew anything about someone tearing up a brush harbor of theirs down near where I lived and I didn't know anything about it, but when my stepfather ran through the cornfield and into the pine thicket, he must have run right into that brush harbor. That would account for the pine needles all over him. Incidentally, my stepfather didn't investigate this accident and he hasn't been bothered by anymore brahma bulls.

"COW"

Early each morning I would lead our cow to Mr. John Horn's pasture for grazing with his cattle. Since we only had a small barn with a stable and no grazing land, Mr. John offered his good hospitality and we appreciated this. I could catch the bus to school from his house and it was only one half mile over there from where we lived. Late every evening I would return to the pasture, place the fiber halter over the cow's head and lead her slowly along the dirt road to our stable. If I rushed her or upset her in any manner she would produce a smaller amount of milk, so I always let her take her own good time.

One evening during the fall of the year, I led her slowly toward home at almost dark. I could see about 100 feet along the road which had a hazy film of dust hovering over it from late evening travelers by car and trucks. About half way home the cow came to a sudden stop and would not budge. We were standing in the middle of the road and she was looking straight at my spine. I remembered Uncle Hoyt saying, "If an animal attempts to charge at you, step briskly aside and the animal will miss because they shut their eyes when they charge." Although our cow didn't have any horns and was called "a muley head", she was still considered dangerous when upset. I stepped briskly aside, but she paid me no attention and kept staring straight ahead with both ears sticking straight out. I turned to look in the same direction, but at that instant she lunged out of the road, across the ditch and down through the cotton field. She ran with every bit of strength in her body and it wasn't long until I was on the ground with her dragging me. The halter broke away and she lost me about 50 feet from the road. As she continued on toward the house at flank speed, I lay there watching the road and wondering what on earth would I tell my mom when the cow didn't give any milk and also, what in the world had she seen that made her act like this. Then I began to see it myself, it was huge to me. About 10 feet tall and 5 feet around. Its shape was almost like that of a huge football cut in half with the middle section near the ground. It was moving along the road at about the speed which I would trot and was making a continuous low muffled rattling sound. The color was light brown and almost blended into the road and overhanging dust. I had quit breathing and don't think my heart was beating. One thing was for sure, I didn't want it to know I was there. I watched it disappear down the road into the dust and darkness then I made my flight for home.

When I arrived, my mother had captured our cow near the barn and was attempting to calm her down. My explanation of what had happened was so garbled and confusing until it became useless, so I gave up and took the beating which always came when the cow didn't give milk.

The next morning after a sleepless night, I again led our cow back to Mr. John's pasture. She had settled down by now, but I was still upset so I straggled along the road looking for tracks of some sort which would have been left by this monster. When I arrived at the location where she left the road dragging me, there was no doubt it had happened and it wasn't a dream.

When I returned that evening from school, my mom told me news had reached there today of Mr. Buck Beard's mules running away with him and his wagon late yesterday about a mile from where we lived. She said he was traveling along the road and only got a glimpse of something which looked like a large brown half football. She said she was sorry for not believing me and would try to find out what it was that I had seen and had scared the cow so bad.

Later that week we were told a fascinating story by Mr. John Horn. It seems that Mr. Clustus Tyner was pulling fardels of corn leaves down near Bond's School for a man which gave him one-fourth of the amount for his labor. He had stacked all these small bundles and tied the stack together. At the end of his day's work, he had gotten under the stack and into the center. He then poked a hole out through one side so he could see and hauled this stack home on his bicycle. Mr. Tyner lived about 2 miles from us and he traveled the main road to his home that night. Later I talked with Mr. Clustus about this and he told me he didn't see any animals or men on the road that night. I told him, "Sir, they were all gone by the time you reached where they would have been."

"BOAT"

During the transition period from grammar to high school at Ila High, all students were required to select or simply be assigned a future membership group of which there were two available. Most of the boys chose the F.F.A. (Future Farmers of America) and the girls selected the F.H.A. (Future Homemakers of America). Those selecting the opposite were considered as fagots (a bundle of sticks) or they were not accepted socially as a good choice of playmate.

Walter Barrett and I readily joined the F.F.A. and was initiated by the administrative staff. We were ordered to walk upon a sheet of galvanized metal while bare footed and blind folded. A member of the staff then turned the crank of a squeaking telephone transformer coil and we didn't let any grass grow under us during our departure from that sheet of metal. Andrew Adams had given me a big chew of Brown Mule while we were robbing the coke machine and I swallowed it in mid-air. To my knowledge, that was my first and last chew of tobacco.

Walter and I didn't join the F.F.A. for the purpose of pursuing a life time of farming, although at the time it seemed to be the only suitable subject available to insure survival in Madison County. We had premeditated plans and this afforded us of a sure opportunity to get hold of vitally needed resources. Almost as soon as we gained entry to the workshop provided for F.F.A. members, we were putting our dream plans into motion. Our indoctrination in the use of tools and machines was brief and we attached our interest to the gas welding instructions as if our lives depended on this trade. Shortly afterwards we obtained a 1940 Ford truck hood from the junk yard, then we found a Chevy Coupe top which had been cut away from the car. We brought these to the workshop and commenced to join the two parts together by gas welding. After many burns to our body and very sore eyes, we succeeded in attaching the hood to the top. It looked like a boat and we could see fish before our eyes, unlike others who were interested in dollars. However, a commissioning test on our prize product proved to be a disappointment when we placed it in the cool waters of a hand made swimming pool at a creek just north of Ila city limits. What we thought to be an award winning welding job turned out to be a shower head when we applied our weight to the boat.

Walter brought some roofing tar from his home and we covered the welded area inside and out with a heavy coat and sure enough it worked. Our boat stayed almost dry, even when we both rode in it. So we set our next part of the plan into motion.

We borrowed a 150 foot trotline from Mr. George

Christian, then shot a rabbit for bait and tied the boat on top of Mr. Barret's 1934 Ford.

Mason Mill Pond was our destination although fishing by trotline or the use of a boat in the pond was prohibited by its owner. The way Walter and I had it figured, someone must have dammed this creek up a thousand years ago and there would be lots of huge catfish in there well worth taking some extra chances of getting caught. We drove the car as close as we could to the lake's upper end and proceeded with boat in hand for another two miles down the creek before reaching a suitable place to camp. We would build a small fire on the creek's edge, then creep into the mouth of the lake under light of a half moon and put the line out in an ideal location. As we approached the lake there was deep mud under the water, which at times buried our legs to the knees. We slipped into the boat and started paddling out to deeper water. The water temperature in the lake was much warmer than it had been in the creek near Ila and it didn't take long to see what was happening to the tar seal. As the tar broke loose it began to stick between our toes and fingers, then it was all over us. By now the water was pouring in through the defective weld and we were rapidly sinking. We decided to take the rabbit and line along with us and abandon the boat. We waited until the boat was under water to avoid noise, but when we stepped out we found an unlimited mud bottom with water over our heads, so we had to fight the mud and swim for our lives. We finally reached the bank of the lake while still clinging to the trotline and sack of cut rabbit. After walking back through the woods to where our small camp fire burned, I noticed we were wearing snow shoes made of dry leaves. The tar had settled all over our bodies and was grabbing hold of everything we came near.

After a while, we decided on an alternate plan. Rather than face defeat we would stretch the trotline full length along the creeks edge and bait all hooks with the rabbit. Walter, being the older and wiser, would take the lead pole and feel his way into the lake at a more solid location. I would bring up the far pole and once in the lake, we would spread out to the lines full length before stobbing it down in the lakes bottom. The agreement was to go into the lake until the water reached our chin and without talking wait for each other to get into position. After I had traveled about 50 yards into the lake the water began running into my mouth, so I stopped. I was sure Walter should be in position by now, because he was an inch shorter than me and I rolled my head slowly to the right to see if I could locate him in the moonlight. About that time there came a tremendous jerk on the trotline, so hard it carried my pole right out of my hands. Then I saw a large white spot on the water just about where Walter should have been and this was followed by splashing with white water spraying up in the moonlight from something very large as it headed straight out into deep water toward the dam. At first I thought, what on earth is Walter doing, then suddenly, I became temporarily paralyzed with fright. As I turned and plowed through the mud bottom with my head under the water and running with every ounce of strength in my body, I knew, Oh God, walter has been eaten by an alligator. I'd heard of them, but never seen one and right then I'd give anything not to see one. When I got clear of the lake, my body was pushing water like a submerged submarine at full speed. I hit that creek at maximum speed and headed toward the camp fire. Right now I needed to get all my wits back, however, get to a safer place first. As I made my approach to the small camp fire, I could see someone moving up ahead of me at a rapid pace through the dim light trickling down the tree branches. When I arrived at the fire, Walter was there. He was white with shock and his face was covered with blood along with the tar. I grabbed him and pulled his head in against my chest while attempting to wipe the blood out of his eyes. I was so glad to see him there alive and after washing away most of the blood from his head and face, we walked hand in hand back to the car. Not much was said in those two miles, because we were both suffering from shock along with deep disappointment and being stuck to our clothes by tar.

When we arrived at Mr. and Mrs. Barrett's house, his mother washed his head and placed iodine over all the wounds which looked like he had been slapped on both sides of the head by a wildcat. The mystery of what had happened couldn't be solved that night, but the following day Uncle Hoyt Adams and Mr. Barrett listened to both our stories and they came to a conclusion of which seemed reasonable. It was a fact, the area of Mason's Mill Pond was a sanctuary for the large whooping crane. From this we could assume that one of these large cranes had made a landing on what he thought was a stump protruding from the water, which in fact, was Walter's head. However, when Walter jerked his head under the water, the crane was taken by surprise and attempted to hold on causing the large claw scratches to Walter's head. What I would have heard and seen was the huge bird trying desperately to get air borne after his stump had disappeared.

"DEJA-VU"

As far back as I can remember, when only a very young child and until this very day, there is a picture planted firmly into my mind. During my childhood I viewed this as possibly a dream I might have had when I was a small baby however, it has no resemblance to the dreams I had in childhood or as an adult. There have been dreams of falling from a cliff or of some huge object falling on me, but these always woke me and later I wouldn't remember the exact manner in which the dream was assembled. Dreams of animals chasing me or of something dreadful happening to a member of my family would linger longer, but none of these became imbedded in my mind to form a complete picture of events over a long period of time. Most all the dreams which I vaguely remember have been related to a particular thought or incident and normally always distinguished the different sexes and voices or sounds were pronounced in a particular pattern.

The picture which I can see day and night never changes and it has never had sound, although the scene as it appears in my mind would have many varieties of sound, plus there would be motion. To fully understand the extent of my concern, you would have to know I was born on farm land and grew up among crops of cotton and corn. The grassy hills covered with trees and valleys with clear running streams in no way resembled this picture, however, it was as clear in my mind then, as it is right now. The people whom I see are definitely human. The difference being there is no definite difference in sex. I also can't make out what my own sex is in the picture. The people are running in panic and are dressed in long robe like garments and have head scarves on, but I can see some of their faces plainly. It appears as if I have stopped to look back or I was traveling in the opposite direction. Many huge chunks of reddish brown stone or mud is falling and rolling about on a cobblestone, narrow street. Straight ahead of me there is a huge arch made of stone and it is crumbling. I can see the large cracks developing and see the dust boiling from what looks like a very old city, but I can't see the huge arch fall. The ground has begun opening and I can see large deep splits in the earth. In this picture I am the same as all others but there is no pain, no thought or no remembrance beyond this point on my mind.

In 1950 I joined the U.S. Navy and during the next several years I had an opportunity to visit many different countries. It was eleven years later, in 1961, when my ship pulled into the harbor of a small city, in the country of Turkey, for a two day good will tour. On the approach and after docking, there was nothing about this place which differed from any other we had visited around the

Mediterranean Sea. Since our crew was on port and starboard duties, I could go on shore the first night in, but would have duty the next. Upon entry to a port in any foreign country, all service men are always briefed in the code of conduct which they must maintain among themselves at all times while ashore. Izmir was no exception and had some added precautions. These were, don't touch any of the many Turkish flags hanging out along the streets and always travel in pairs. Being my first visit to Turkey and since I probably would never come back that way, I wanted to go ashore even if only to look or shop and just to get off the ship after a long cruise. A sailor from High Point, N.C. wanted to travel with me, so we set out to see the town together. We caught a cab into town and along the way I saw carts being pulled by donkeys, although there were lots of cars and trucks. As we entered the main part of town, the streets were packed with people and suddenly I felt very sick. I asked the driver to stop and although he couldn't understand or speak English, he got my message. I stood there on the narrow cobblestone street for several minutes as I scanned the town around me from building to building. My friend asked me if I had a problem and I told him I felt faint and sick, that I'd be o.k. in a minute. The truth was I couldn't hear him talking now, because suddenly I knew where I was. Some of the city had been renewed but there before my eyes was a large part of the picture which had been clear in my mind for all these years. The blocks, stones and shapes were identical as I had always seen them. The renewed portions of the city had taken almost the same shape and looked to be no more than 100 years old. After finally pulling myself together I told my friend I'd like to go in this specific direction to see what we could find and after walking for about five minutes, we came to what once was the only market in the city. Most of it had crumbled to the ground and more modern markets had been set up around the old location. I sat down on one of the stones and asked my friend if this scene was familiar to him. He replied, "Heck no, I've never seen anything like this place." So I asked him if he would like to see the coliseum. He did, but wanted to take a cab and I told him it wasn't far. I'd show him the way. He said, "You gotta be kidding me." So I told him to come on. I weaved through alleys and crossed streets in a manner which would cause a local resident to get lost and when I pointed to the mostly collapsed coliseum, my friend said, "you've been here before". I told him I believed so, as a matter of fact, I'm sure I have been here before. I knew he thought I had visited this city by ship before, so I didn't explain to him what I had seen in my mind. I never visited Izmir Turkey again and to tell the truth I have a profound fear to go back there. Only one other man ever heard this story and his name was Vic Crowley from Birmingham, England. I told him about this in 1981 and he said the French have a specific name for this picture, but couldn't remember what it was.

"MANIFEST"

In the late 50's and early 60's the best and safest mode of transportation seemed to be the passenger train and I utilized this to the maximum extent for travel. I had never considered flying and had never been on board any type of aircraft until I received orders in 1960 to the U.S.S. Independence CVA-62 which was deployed someplace in the Middle East. I packed my sea bag at Norfolk, Va. and caught a DC3 out of Little Creek headed for, who knows where. Back then you followed your orders and kept your mouth shut. What you weren't told wasn't any of your business in the first place. The huge prop driven plane didn't seem to be in any hurry once it was air borne and there was plenty of cold box lunches for everyone, so I just sat and relaxed on my maiden flight. After about six hours of this, I began to ask around to see if anyone knew where we were going and a man told me we would land in Newfoundland. I would like to see this place in the winter and see if there was some connection to its name, however, when the props were reversed on a snow covered runway, I knew the name had nothing to do with it. We had been in flight for eight hours, so the pilot allowed everyone to leave and get hot coffee from the airport diner. After refueling, we loaded up and were off again to, who knows where. After another six hours I began asking around again about our destination and was told we would land on an island in the Azores for fuel. Sure enough, after eight hours flying time we landed on an island and refueled. This time we didn't leave the plane, but we were issued a new batch of cold box lunches. By now these bologna sandwiches were getting good and I had already collected twelve oranges. The way I had it figured, our next stop should be at the aircraft carrier and I could get a good shower and lay flat down for a change. After about five more hours I began to see land up ahead, but it wasn't what I had expected. It looked like we were flying right out over a hugh desert as we left the sea and I began asking questions again. According to what I could gather we were going to land in Morocco and that's where the plane would leave us. After landing we loaded our sea bags in a truck and were hauled to a group of quonset huts on what looked like some sort of military base. The men there were dressed in several different types of uniforms and I learned we were at an International peace keeping camp. We unloaded the truck and at dinner a short time later, I met men from the French, Italian, and British Army. All seemed in good spirits and eager to meet new comers. When we returned from the evening meal we were told not to unpack because we wouldn't be there long, so I opened my sea bag to get some clean shorts and a towel. To my surprise, every item of clothing in my sea bag was slippery to my fingers, so I removed the neat stacks to investigate. When I packed the bag in Norfolk, I had placed a large box of Tide in the center among my wool uniforms so it wouldn't get damaged and it wasn't broken open, but there wasn't a sign of dust inside the box. The vibration of the aircraft had caused the soap powder to leave the box and super saturate every stitch of clothing I had, except those on my body. There wasn't any washing facilities here, nor a place to hang anything for drying, so I felt kinda sick. I thought to myself, "what a mess and all over a $.57 box of soap". I discussed the problem with a man who was to bunk above in the double bunks and he suggested I shower and wear my old shorts until we could look around the next day. I didn't have any luck the following day, so I washed two pairs of shorts in a small sink which overflowed with suds. After several rinses I hung them over the open window seal to dry and while I was at lunch, they disappeared. The huts were equipped with steam heat, so I washed another pair and dried them on the heater while I watched. After being there three days and being told each day not to unpack, I had decided to take a chance. I knew I had to get the soap out of these clothes and the sooner the better. I asked a friend to help me stand watch and obtained some line from the French camp. I strung the line from corner to corner of the quonset huts on the outside. In Morocco there was plenty of sunshine, although the weather was cold and if I had just a few hours to work with, I would rinse out and dry most of my sea bag. I began to wash one item at a time and run out to hang it out on the line while my friend stood watch. I worked from six in the morning until noon, then relieved my friend so he could go eat. I didn't get a meal that day and at 2 p.m. we received word to load up for a flight out. In a panic I grabbed all the wet clothing and stashed them back into my sea bag. Now the bag was twice as heavy to carry, but these people weren't kidding. We headed to the runway and was loaded onto an R-5D aircraft. After take off from Morocco the floor of the plane got very cold and we were issued G.I. blankets. The pilot said the small planes heaters had failed and he would land in Paris to see if the situation could be corrected. At one time while flying over the mountain, a crew member told me the temperature of the plane's floor, where my feet were, was below zero. He told me to wrap my feet in a portion of the blanket to prevent frost bite. By the time the plane landed at Paris, I was completely enclosed by the blanket and was trying to keep my body warm with my breath. I wasn't allowed to get off the plane so I decided to stay enclosed in the blanket to avoid freezing to death. After about an hour, we left Paris and the plane seemed to go straight up when it left the runway. I didn't see any need in trying to bust a person's ear drums like that and also the prop driven engines sounded like they almost stalled. When the plane tapered off, I came out from under the blanket long enough to look out and I saw we had climbed up and over a very tall mountain. About the time I got myself comfortably back under the blanket, someone tapped on my head. I uncovered and saw a crew member standing there with an Alaskan fur jacket on trying to hand me a frozen box lunch. There was no way I could eat frozen food with my body temperature this low, so I simply ignored him and recovered my head. Several hours later the plane landed in Naples, Italy and I was told to get off. By now I was having a hard time parting with the blanket and once outside, I could barely walk. Some men loaded my sea bag along with other cargo onto a truck and told me to ride in the carryall with them. They noticed my teeth chattering and body shaking but didn't say anything and this made me happy, because I couldn't have talked anyway. They carried me across Naples to a receiving center which had a very simple setup for transients. You checked in at a desk and was told to take one of the two double bunks around the corner and this was the best thing that had happened to me in the last nine hours. At least now I could feel real heat around me and was beginning to thaw when two men brought in my sea bag. They told the man at the desk someone had shipped a bag full of ice from Morocco. The wet clothing had frozen at several degrees below zero and had split the bag open on one side. I walked over, took the bag in tow and dragged it into the room alongside my bunk while everyone watched. I thought, I'm tired, hungry and cold. I took off the wool uniform which I had been wearing for over a week and acting like I could care less, jumped into one of the bottom bunks and covered up. It wasn't long before I went to sleep, although the office noise would normally bother me. It was almost 4 a.m. when I had got to bed and I had no idea what was in store for tomorrow, except I knew every day reveille went at 6 a.m. sharp with no exceptions. I couldn't have been asleep over thirty minutes when I suddenly woke and realized I was being smothered to death by a large mattress over my face and a heavy object on top of the mattress. The breath had been knocked out of me when this thing hit my whole body and I couldn't breathe inward. I fought for my life and as suddenly as it had happened, the heavy object was gone and I sent the mattress flying through the air. At that time I could see a man standing near my bunk in his shorts and there wasn't anything in the bunk above me. Another man ran into the small room from the office asking what had happened. No one seemed to know right away, but after we got the lights turned on, I could see that someone had removed all the connecting links from the center of the top bunk springs. The big man standing in his shorts was also a transient and had arrived after me. He had been assigned to the top bunk and like myself was very tired, naturally when he jumped up into that bunk it had come flying down through the missing center portion and directly on top of my body. I was assured it wasn't meant to happen this way and the man was assigned to sleep in the other bottom bunk. Even at that he lifted the mattress and inspected the springs before lying down. Early the following morning we were issued a theater ticket and told to go next door and present the ticket for our breakfast. The small diner was operated by Italian government employees on U.S. payroll and the food was cooked American style. All people eating in the diner were employed by the U.S. Naval Supply Depot and they were Italians, but most of them spoke fair English. I talked with one of the employees, who had joined our table for breakfast, and he could get my entire bag of clothing rinsed and dried by his wife for 6,000 lira ($5.00) so I took him up on the deal. We went to the office and got the bag of clothes, which had started to form a large puddle of water beside my bunk. The Italian asked a question about this water but I told him it was a long story and I didn't want to talk about it. The other transient left for his ship, which was docked in the harbor at Naples, and I was told to stand by for a flight out to the Independence. The personnel man said he would get me on a cargo flight and I would land on the carrier. He told me no one knew where she was nor did he know when the plane would come in, so the best thing for me to do would be to stay ready to go 24 hours each day. I spent the next two days folding and repacking my clothing as the Italian delivered it. Not only did his wife get the soap and mildew out, but she pressed everything including my shorts and sewed up the ripped sea bag. By now I had made good friends with the Italian government employee and we were talking to each other on a first name basis. Tony drove a navy exchange sandwich truck and it was his job to make sales to sailors and employees at the docks and fleet landing. He asked me to ride along with him because the sailors would sometimes try to get the food from him without paying. I talked with the personnel man about this and he thought it was a good idea, so he issued me a set of orders to ride shotgun on the Gedunk truck as shore patrol. Actually, he had been trying to come up with something to get me out of his hair anyway. I had been asking about the plane every thirty minutes and I was very much concerned about where my pay and medical records were. When I left Little Creek, Virginia, I only had my baggage and my orders in a brown envelope along with $32.00 cash. Now I had $27.00 left and was running out of cigarettes and soap. Knowing how impossible it was to get cash from the navy without my pay record had me a bit worried and no one had any idea how long

I'd have to wait in Naples. I would be very careful with the money I had and only buy the absolute necessities, like cigarettes. During my first run with Tony I learned several things about Naples which were going to be a big help to me in the days to come. First of all, when you are with an Italian in Italy let him purchase everything you want to buy. His price for things, like espresso coffee or beer, were four times cheaper than they would charge me and he got better service. U. S. cigarettes were only available at the small diner and I couldn't save on them but could get him a carton once in a while and he could save on them or sell them at a profit on the black market. At first I didn't like the espresso coffee but later, I almost became addicted to the stuff. The round trip each day along the docks and to fleet landing almost consumed the normal working hours for Tony since he would make several stops to get coffee or shoot the breeze with his friends. Many times we would stop to observe a fight going on between two Italians over a fender bender, just to see which one won the case. All accidents in Italy are settled by the drivers on the street as it occurs and normally without any intervention of the police. Tony became a good friend of mine and after my money ran out, he began loaning me some of his lira. There were 1200 lira to $1.00 and with him along to do my buying, each dollar I borrowed went a long way. After about three weeks, I realized I had borrowed over 18,000 lira from Tony and began to worry about how I would repay him. One night I got an idea of a scheme which might work and since Tony loved to drink wine, vino in Italy, I might be able to pay him off in wine, If he would help me. He could understand American language real well so I told him about my idea and how he fit in as an important partner. He knew where all the pubs were and these were always loaded with Italian laborers during the early evening hours. They would stop in and enjoy a bottle or two of their favorite wine each day after work and this would be the ideal time to reap the harvest. Tony would enter the pub about 15 minutes before me and I would come in as a total stranger. No one would know we knew each other and the way I had it figured, we wouldn't have to hit the same pub twice. I needed some civilian clothes so as not to arouse the shore patrol, which would prowl about town if a ship came in, so Tony bought me an outfit suitable for the occasion. Tony's job would be to enter first and take up a position at the bar. After a few minutes I would enter and position myself where I had full view of Tony at all times, but be as far from him as possible. I would attempt to strike up a conversation with one or two of the Italians and if I succeeded I would introduce three identical coins, which I'd place on the bar at about three inches apart. Then I would bet the Italian a bottle of wine

I could tell him which coin he touched with my head turned and eyes closed or if he preferred he could blindfold me. If he took my bet, Tony would light up a cigarette and in a smoke filled Italian pub with 30 men chattering, smoking and drinking, no one would even notice Tony. Several things could happen while my eyes were shut and Tony would have to watch close because he knew I didn't have the slightest idea which coin would be touched. The easiest bet would be if one man touched one coin, even if he moved it into another location, but I knew they would increasingly make it harder so I covered every possible move I could think of with Tony before arriving. Sure enough the first bottle bet went well by the Italian who was doing the touching telling his friend to cover my eyes with their hands after he turned my back to the three coins. When they were ready, I turned and lifted one coin to my left. I placed it to my nose and smelled it while at the same time glancing at Tony. Tony placed the cigarette in the middle of his mouth and took a drag. I laid the left coin back on the bar and lifted the middle one to my nose. Tony didn't move his cigarette and I laid the center one back on the bar. I lifted the coin on my right to my nose and Tony again did not move. I lay the right one down and lifted the middle one, telling the Italian, this was the one he had touched. He was shocked but had the bartender bring me a bottle to pay his debt. Suddenly, I had drawn a crowd but the first better wanted to get even, so he asked me to bet him once more and I accepted. This time they placed a black wool stocking cap over my face and held my hands over my eyes after turning my back to the coins. When they were ready, they removed the stocking cap and turned me around. I began picking up the coins as before but Tony did not raise his cigarette to his mouth, so after I smelled all three coins, I told the Italian he had not touched any of the coins. Up came another bottle of wine and now I really had their attention. Next came a two man team, they bet me two bottles I couldn't do it for them. I accepted and one of them led me to a dingy rest room. He placed me inside and he remained between me and the door. The two of them yelled back and forth to each other in Italian, until finally I was led back to the bar. As I picked up the left coin, Tony placed the cigarette in the left side of his mouth. As I picked up the middle one he placed it in the middle of his mouth and as I lifted to smell the right one he placed it in the right side of his mouth. I looked at the Italian and told him he had touched all three coins. Up came two more bottles of wine and you could see the firm belief in the men's eyes, yet they weren't about ready to give up. These two men switched chores and the other led me to the rest room. This time they blindfolded me and again the man stood in the door, but they didn't yell at each other, maybe figuring I could understand their language and possibly got a clue from what they had said. After a while he removed the blindfold and led me back to the bar. When I reached for the coin on the left, the other man stopped me and pointed to the one on the right, I lifted it and smelled but Tony didn't move. I asked the man which one next and he pointed to the left. When I lifted the coin Tony placed the cigarette in the left side of his mouth and when I lifted the middle coin, Tony took a drag from the middle of his mouth. I looked at the man and told him he had touched two coins, one to the left and the middle one. Up came two more bottles of wine but these two fellows were upset. Now, I had six bottles of wine on the bar and the last two which bet wanted to confer with some friends. In a few minutes they returned and the same two bet me six bottles of wine I couldn't do it again. I asked the bartender for a rag and wiped off the three coins as if it was of any importance then I accepted their bet. This time both men stayed behind and three others led me to the rest room. They each stood directly in front of me, with the rest room door closed and looked straight into my eyes as if to confuse me. After a long time they led me back to the bar and as I lifted the left coin they didn't stop me as before but I noticed Tony was giving me another type of signal which we didn't discuss. He was shutting his eyes twice, then opening them wide, then shutting them twice again. I hadn't smelled the coin and told them I was confused and asked if I could start over. They approved so I again lifted the left coin, hoping Tony would know I had caught on. He didn't move at all on that one and when I lifted the middle coin he placed the cigarette in the right side of his mouth then removed it and placed it right back in the right side. I lay the coin down and pointed to the man on my left. I told him both men had touched a coin, he had touched the middle coin and the man on the right had touched the right coin. We now had 12 bottles of wine and I hadn't noticed the two neatly dressed men who had been observing from over near the front door. They walked through the crowd and straight up to me. Every one else gave way to them and I could see from the expression on Tony's face he didn't want to be playing any games with these two men. I knew something was wrong but I felt it would be even worse if these laborers found out what we had been doing. One of the men asked me, in almost perfect American language, if I could detect things by smell. I told him that was my game and he said,"I will bet you 100,000 lira you can't tell me which of us touched the other shoulder and which shoulder he touched. This was an easy one but I was afraid of a trick and didn't have money to cover the bet, however, I told him I'd bet the 12 bottles of wine and he agreed. One of the other men was told to blindfold me and turn my back to the two men. In a second they were ready, as if they didn't have time to waste, so the blindfold was removed and I turned to face them. Their backs were toward Tony and I knew we could get this reversed and mess up, so I asked them to step aside and told the bartender to give me a small glass of wine before I did this one. They agreed because I had a lot at stake and I moved against the bar. I asked them to face me and place both hands out in front of them. Tony was now in a position where he could give the correct signal. I looked like a fool smelling each of these guy's fingers as they giggled but even worse pulling them over near to me to smell each of their shoulders. When I lifted the first man's hand Tony had his cigarette in the right side of his mouth. He kept it in the same place as I finished smelling all fingers so I knew the man on Tony's right has done the touching. That narrowed it down to either the right or the left shoulder of the man on Tony's left. When I smelled the shoulders of the man on the right, Tony didn't move and when I pulled the man on the left to me, Tony again took a drag from his cigarette after he placed it in the right side of his mouth. After the smelling ordeal was over I told the man on the right he had touched the other man's right shoulder. The one who had placed the bet pulled out a wad of lira and told the bartender to place 12 bottles of wine in a sack and to sack the 12 already on the bar. Both men showed me some sort of badges and told me to come with them. They said they were a sort of police and helped me carry the wine to their car. I had ridden down there with Tony so he came out and followed us to a police station. After a long closed door session with the one they called Inspector, the police placed me in a room with a real super duper interrogator who couldn't see through his glasses apparently, because he was always looking at me, either from above or below the lenses. I told him I was an American service man and was playing a guessing game. He wasn't convinced but let me go after I filled out a form which told them where I was staying in Naples. He called the two police which brought me in and they carried me to the Navy depot, with Tony following. Once there, the police gave me my 12 bottles of wine, but reneged on their bet and kept the other 12 bottles. Tony said, they either thought I was some sort of kook or else they believed I could be of some use to them. I gave him the wine but he wouldn't take it unless I came to his home and drank some with his family, so I checked the office about a flight out and there was none. I met Tony's family for the first time and they didn't speak much English, so he acted as interpreter. His wife was a fat woman and they had six nice children, the oldest not more than 12. We drank some together at his home and like all house parties, they end up finishing in a club so he drove me to a place near his home. We had a lot to drink there and I couldn't get over the shape of one girl's hairdo. It looked like a huge black hay stack and was about ten times out of proportion to her body. I kept watching her and when I passed her table, I patted on top of the stack with my hand. I only tapped her softly and the thing caved in making her a large black Chinese sun bonnet. She jumped up and slapped my face faster than lightening, yelled Italian words which sounded dirty, and disappeared toward the door. It made some of the fellows in there angry also and Tony decided I was ready to go back to the depot and hit the sack. The next day I felt awful and each time I drank water I was sick again. I never have cared for wine since.

A few days later I got placed on a manifest list to Barcelona, Spain aboard another R-5D aircraft. The personnel man told me I couldn't be bumped by cargo because a manifest is the list of a positive load. I boarded at noon along with 14 other men and a bunch of cargo which the crewman said was for the Independence. This time I felt sure to reach the aircraft carrier, get paid and settle down in my job again. We were airborne about an hour and started descending over the Mediterranean Sea. I thought, surely this can't be Spain in such a short time, because it was just across the lake from Morocco and as we turned to line up the runway, I could see the huge No.62 right underneath us. We were coming in almost directly over the flight deck of the U.S.S. Independence, which was at anchor about four miles out of the harbor at Palermo, Sicily. Everybody makes mistakes so I was sure someone gave me bum information about Barcelona. I knew for sure it wasn't a mistake when I saw the carrier back there and that was where I was supposed to go. The plane landed on an isolated runway and I waited for someone to tell me to get off but no one came. After a while I went up front to find out what was going on and found no one there to ask. I hung my head out the door and asked the lone sailor working with some soldiers where they were carrying that cargo. He said,"To the Independence." so I let him know I was supposed to go too. He said I'd better hurry, because they were fixing to leave. I climbed down the small ladder and into the belly of the plane. There I found my sea bag, dragged it out and loaded it onto the truck. I climbed in back with several soldiers, while the sailor and one soldier doing the driving sat up front. It didn't take long to figure out these weren't U.S. service men and none of them understood the American language. The truck passed through a small town and stopped near the bay. A large personnel boat was waiting and I climbed on board carrying my sea bag. The boat coxswain didn't say anything to me, although he hadn't been told about me coming, but from his look I could see he was concerned. We pulled alongside the long high sea ladder at the aircraft carrier and I proceeded to the top. Although I was carrying a full sea bag and the coxswain hadn't asked me any questions, it was a different tale when I reached the quarter deck. I broke out every item of identification I had along with my orders and that wasn't enough. I guess, no matter who you are, if you're reporting on board an aircraft carrier, you better personally let someone know you are coming. I was frisked, then turned over to the ships master-at-arms, who emptied my sea bag. Finally they were convinced enough that I belonged there, then they took me below and began showing me where I would sleep and eat. The next morning I reported back to the master-at-arms and they delivered me to my division officer. For a change, I found someone who knew I was supposed to be there, because he said he had received my records over a month ago and had been looking for me. He showed me my work station and introduced me to my chief in charge. He was expecting me too, but about an hour later, we were all in the department heads office trying to explain where I came from. I simply couldn't understand this mess and the department head said, "Let me put some light on the picture for all of you. When this man boarded the plan in Naples, he was on a manifest to Barcelona, Spain. A manifest is mandatory when transporting military personnel through foreign countries and the manifest destination of each and everything aboard that carrier must be received at that point. If it leaves one country and doesn't arrive in the country of destination, it is not taken for granted, but becomes a fact that somebody or something is roaming around out there loose in a totally unauthorized place with no visa, passport, or any other means of reason for being there. In this particular situation, manifested cargo and a man were missing when the plane landed in Barcelona, so the pilots report becomes an international incident." I told him what happened and he said he would try to clear it up, but I would still have to go to see the captain. I was taken before the four striper the next day, and he said,"This ship may never have gone to Barcelona, but you are not to violate a military manifest again." And I never did it again.

"SCUTTLE BUTT"

The ship had left Naples, Italy early in the morning on high tide and at a glance around the decks, one could readily see the sickness of hangover in many of the sailors eyes. We had been in port for three days to pick up some fresh provisions along with two new sailors out of recruit training before sailing on into the Mediterranean Sea to join other elements of the sixth fleet. My ship was an amphibious force flag command vessel which carried about 620 officers and men, plus flag units when we were deployed into combat zones. Most all the crews quarters were located below the main deck and some were below the ships water line. At about 9 a.m. that morning, I received a call from the police petty officer (petty officer in charge of division environment and conduct) and he wanted to report a clogged scuttle butt (water fountain). I logged the report and glanced around the shop to see who I might have available to answer the call. One man available was a red haired 2nd class pipe fitter who was highly respected and fully capable of performing most all types of trouble calls. He was superior in his sobriety, honesty and devotion to his duties. I assigned him the call and instructed him to return with details if there were any unusual problems. After a few minutes he returned and said, "Chief you gotta see this." He said one of the sailors had returned sick from liberty in Naples and had upchucked spaghetti and meatballs into the scuttle butt. I called the police petty officer of the division and told him when he removed that mess and if then the drain was still clogged, I'd send a man to work on it. He said, " O.K." and when I didn't get a return call during the day, I assumed the problem was solved and marked it off in the trouble log. This particular berthing compartment was located two decks down below the water line of the ship and any water from sanitary units drained from there into a sump located four more decks down into the auto hole. All below the water line sanitary lines drained to this sump which held several tons of used fresh water, then when it reached a certain level, the float would energize an electric motor which pumped it until dry. All sanitary drainage from above the water line was directed through piping to one of the ships sides and drained out into the sea through scuppers. The men living in the compartment with the clogged scuttle butt were operational personnel and worked directly for the operations officer, who normally was the ships executive officer, known to everyone as the "XO", or the next in line of authority to the captain.

Three days later I received a call from my division officer asking if someone called several days ago about a stopped up drain in the operations division compartment. I answered, "Yes" and before any further explanation, he sharply told me to go down there personally and resolve the problem. I grabbed the red haired pipe fitter and proceeded rapidly to the clogged scuttle butt. By now the spaghetti and meatballs had settled down into the drain and left about a half inch of mess stuck to the sides of the catch water which had dried and the stench was awful. We used scrapers and rags to remove as much of the mess as possible, then we got our heads together on how to unstop something that would normally never get clogged, therefore it wasn't equipped with unstopping features. Finally, I decided to remove the plug on the vent pipe and use a little squirt of CO2 from a nearby 15 pound fire extinguisher. This was against regulations because the liquid CO2 would expand 600 times its volume in vapor when it was released into the atmosphere. The fire extinguisher is equipped with a fiber glass horn which protects the user from freezing his hand and also absorbs the expansion. I told the pipe fitter to stand on the wet rags in the center of the scuttle butt drain and push down from the huge steel beam above his head. He was somewhat reluctant but finally climbed up on the rags and packed them down good and tight. I removed the fiber glass horn from the CO2 bottle and placed the hose inside the drain pipe. I asked the pipe fitter if he was ready and when he shook his head, I pulled the trigger to release the CO2. There was a swift, tremendous explosion and I was flying across the slick steel compartment floor. After untangling myself from the bunk, about twenty feet from the scuttle butt, I realized I hadn't turned loose of the CO2 bottle while in flight. I hurried through the white cloud of carbon dioxide to find the pipe fitter still standing as I had left him, on top of the scuttle butt. His arms were up against the steel beam and there was spaghetti and meat and all other kinds of mess hanging off his nose, chin, eye brows, and under his arm pits. The mess had splattered against the ceiling in a ten foot diameter arc. The rags had blown out from around his feet in small bits and up the inside of his pants legs clear to his belt line. He began climbing down slowly with his arms still extended upwards and I gave him plenty of room. I had never heard him curse so I won't repeat what he was saying as he climbed the ladder leading out of the compartment. Afterwards, I replaced the vent cap and stowed the CO2 bottle. A check of the drain proved it was cleaned out, so I went to where the pipe fitter was taking a shower. I stood outside and asked him not to tell about me using the CO2. He said he didn't care if I used an atomic bomb the next time, because he would never, never be with me to unclog another scuttle butt anyway.

Later that evening, I went to the lounge where several upper grade petty officers would gather to play pinochle.

There I talked with the ships medic and he told me they had received two unexplained casualties during the afternoon. He said two new men were working in the auto hole and had been injured. One had a broken arm and the other had received a concussion. According to the medic their story was unbelievable and he was sure they had gone crazy. When he told me the reported time of the incident, I asked if I could speak with them and he told me which beds they were in at the ships infirmary. As I arrived at the infirmary, the duty medic told me the young man with the concussion was under sedation but I could talk with the one who had the broken arm. The young man told me the two of them had been put in the auto hole to chip paint around rust spots three days ago. There had been no supervisor to check with since this place was six decks down, the only way in or out being up straight ladders and though small holes. The anchor chains were rolling about in the two large hause pipes which passed through the auto hole and there was very few lights down there. After three days of chipping, the two young men had gotten acquainted since they hadn't seen anyone come down, they had sat on a truck hood and began discussing their pasts. He said both of them had decided this was all a scary mistake and they were ready to go home to mother. Suddenly about 2 p.m., a white genie began coming out of one of the pipes and they could hear talking and groaning sounds coming from underneath them. He said he knew they were in the bottom of the ship and any such sounds would be coming from the ocean. Both young men panicked at the same time and injured each other trying to get up the ladder and through the water tight man hole. After one man broke his arm, the other young man with the concussion climbed six decks out and sent help. I told him I believed this had something to do with a sonar unit located on the bottom of the ship and at times it would make these sounds. The fact is, when that CO2 exploded in the pipe it came to the sump and made those sounds, so this was one case that was never resolved on my ship.

"FLARE"

One of the most dreaded cruises in a sailor's career is the shake down trips he will make to Guantanimo Bay, Cuba. Each and every U.S. warship operating in the eastern hemisphere will at one time or another be scheduled to undergo this simulated combat readiness exercise. I wasn't a new comer to this zone and had played war games here several times before, so when I arrived on a sea plane tender I already knew what to expect. Although this was not a liberty port of sorts, the war games normally ceased on Saturday night and if it was your turn for liberty you could go ashore and visit the all male small Navy base on Sunday. The base offered several sorts of recreation, such as baseball, swimming, drinking beer and fishing. Only one brand of beer could be bought at the small club and it was called Hautey, which featured a one eyed Indian on the label. After about two in that temperature, you knew why the Indian had only one eye. Even at your best, it was hard to return to your ship without at least one black eye. At one time when I was trying to make it back through the woods to fleet landing, I fell asleep along the way and when I awoke my wallet was gone. That day I had carried six U.S. war Bonds ashore in an effort to cash them for money and they had gone with my wallet. Three years later I received the same bonds back, someone had mailed them to the Dept. of Defense in Washington, D.C. and they had located me. One night after the liberty boat had left the landing headed back to the ships with a load of sailors, one jumped in the water and began swimming away. An officer on the liberty boat, yelled,"Man overboard", and the sailor in the water yelled back,"Where is he sir, I'll get him". If you counted the good times and bad times, I suppose there were more good than bad, but that's only one man's opinion.

During the day all ships within the fleet would chase submarines, shoot at dummy targets, and occasionally mess up and shoot at each other, but usually all but a few would return to the deep water channel and drop anchor about 300 yards apart. As far as you could see in the wide long channel were destroyers, destroyer escorts, tankers and mine sweepers. Outside of the bay in deeper water were the aircraft carriers, battleships and heavy cruisers. After dark all ships would go into a darken ship exercise which normally lasted for two to three hours. During this time all battle stations above the main deck of each ship would be at general quarters. All sailors involved with gunnery would man their battle stations in full battle dress and chase one little single prop plane with all guns available as the pilot would try to elude them. During this exercise the fire control technician would reset their Gyro's and prepare for the next day of firing. Infra red sighting devices were checked for accuracy and the gunners would simulate chase tomorrow, but most of the black shoe's were free to roam about the ship. Those sailors who worked in the engine rooms and most which worked below the ships main deck were referred to by the name of black shoes because they would track oil over the Boatswain mates clean decks and stayed in trouble with the sailor which lived out in the light and fresh air. I was considered to be a reformed black shoe since I wasn't directly attached to engine rooms but was responsible for below decks damage control. I enjoyed the night exercises because it allowed a rest from the long hard day and you could stand out on the quite dark main deck and get some fresh air for a change. As I stood on the main deck near the stern one night I heard a familiar voice call my name. It was my division officer and he was one of the greatest officers I've ever known. He was a W-4 Warrant and had come up through the enlisted ranks which gave him experience far beyond any officer out of the academy and he was a man you could talk with. The ships were all under complete darkness and were playing their war games, so he suggested we get our fishing tackle and try to pick up a cudda. Both of us enjoyed fishing and often fished together and had good luck. We were in Barracuda territory and I liked the suggestion so we went into the ship and got our 6.0 Penn. Senator reels which carried 60 pound test lines and would hold a 100 pound fish if you handled him right. After getting set up on the stern, we went forward along the ships side until we were above the garbage grinder. Many small fish hung around the overboard discharge from the garbage grinder and we needed two to use on our large rigs. Using treble hooks we snatched until we had caught two small mullets. We placed them in a small pail of water and returned to our fishing rigs on the stern. I hooked mine just below the top fin and lowered it into the water. It began swimming aft and out from the ships stern into the bay. We were having good luck keeping the two small fish apart because his was swimming forward toward the ships bow and out into the bay. As I let more line go, I could feel the small fish pull gently and occasionally make a few small jerks. Both fish had plenty of life and we felt sure we'd catch at least one Barracuda in this pitch darkness. I watched the sparks shooting out of the exhaust all around the little one prop plane's engine as he came shooting across above the ship and I could hear the swirling of large guns swinging on target. My division officer didn't talk much when he was concentrating on a good catch so I always kept quiet too. It was so dark I couldn't see him anyway so I kept easing my line out while feeling of the spool to judge about 200 yards. Once out that far I would still have 100 yards to fight the fish with, and most likely at that distance the mullet wouldn't return and get tangled in the other line. Suddenly, my division officer's voice broke the silence and he suggested we go into the Hanger Bay for a quick smoke (smoking or any light on deck during night combat is strictly prohibited and a minor offense means a court martial, a major offense and you are shot.) I agreed and set my pole down on the ships deck and set the drag. As I started with him to the hanger, he asked if I had tied my pole to the life line. He said," you better go back and tie it off good because a Barracuda will jerk it right over the side". After feeling my way back along the life line to my pole I realized I didn't have anything to tie the pole off with. I didn't carry a handkerchief and my belt wouldn't work so I started feeling around along the life line and main deck because there normally was always a loose piece of line laying about the edge of the ship where it was blown up by the wind. Sure enough there was one and it was tied in a neat bow knot to the life line. That confused me the way it was tied off but it was about the right size cord I needed and I could think of no reason for it being here other than adrift. I followed it back a few feet and it went through the chock and over into the stern lookouts station. This was where a young sailor stood on duty wearing a set of head phones on during all hours when the ship was steaming. I had seen him there many times but never gave it much thought and never asked what his duties were. I looked over and around the chock but couldn't see anything in this darkness so I wrapped the small cord around my wrist and gave it a sharp jerk intending on breaking it. To my surprise, it gave way very easily and I realized the low thump sound which came from the other end was a set of points closing and that might mean trouble. Before my brain could function with another thought there came a loud hissing sound and white fire spewed 25 feet into the air. It lit up the whole world making every ship around come into view and as I jumped over the chock to grab hold of this thing I could see ten thousand big eyes looking at me. My heart had stopped beating as I lunged back over the chock running wildly about the ship trying to find a hole to poke this thing in. Some men came running toward me to help, but turned and ran for their lives when I tried to give it to them. I struck it against the ships deck but it pushed me back and the ship's sides had white fire rolling off like Naples, Italy on new year's night. It was swishing and swirling and I was afraid to turn loose. I put it against the ship, bottom down, and tried to stand on the hole where the white fire was shooting from but it just umbrellared around me and threw me to the ships deck. I grabbed the fire hose and got after it with a 2 1/2 inch stream of water but it went flying down the deck one way and the force of 200 P.S.I. of water coming through the 2 1/2 inch hose sent me flying the other way. Faintly, I could hear my division officer yelling over all the other commotion and he was telling me to grab it and hold it. There hadn't been any problem holding it, my problem was getting rid of it, however I chased it down and lay flat on the deck holding it as it spewed white fire out over the bay. As I lay there, I saw the small single prop plane come over and I could see the pilot in there laughing. My division officer ran up to my side and began looping a line around the thing. On the other end of the short line he had attached a ten pound piping flange and he ran with it to the ships side and dropped the thing into the bay. Every light on every ship was on now and I had caused our entire ships crew to gather on the stern. My division officer came back and lifted me off the deck and walked with me slowly over to the ships side. I didn't much care about the scene down there at the bottom of the bay, but he began pointing out the different types of sharks which had come to investigate the light. It now lit up a 50 foot diameter circle in the blue water and there were hammer heads, browns, blues, sawbills, and many other types of sharks and fish I didn't recognize. Another sailor said he would reel in my line and bring my rig to the damage control central office where I was directed to go with my division officer. My ships captain and "XO" were arriving from the admirals house on the naval station and they would be calling for me soon, so my division officer said he would go up and talk to them first. After he left a gunners mate came in and said I had set off a four stage phosphorus flare equipped with 15 minute stages. He said it was used for night rescue of a man overboard and would have been thrown overboard by the man I had seen standing back there when we were steaming. My division officer called and told me to come to the captain's quarters and as I made my way slowly through the ship in my soaked clothing, I could see that every place I stepped there was a bright white shoe print. When I entered the captain's cabin, I knew there would be nothing short of a general court martial, however, he told me to relax for a moment and settle myself down. He said he could hear my heart beating all the way to his desk. Then he began laughing and pointed for me and my division officer to leave. As I walked away I could hear the "XO" join in the laughter and my division officer said he told them what had happened. The next day the plan of the day directed the crew not to pull on any neatly attached cords around the ship.

"COMPANY COMMANDER"

When I arrived at the Great Lakes Naval Training Center in February 1964, I was issued the traditional red angulette and the title of company commander. Just over 14 years ago, I had taken my own training in this camp and until this day can still see my company commander's face. I can never forget my company commander nor will I every forget the days of my basic training. By this memory, I knew I was undertaking one of the most important jobs of my life and one which many men would remember my expressions of anger and happiness. The same old barracks were still in use at Camp Berry and Moffat but camps Porter and Dewey had been removed and replaced with beautiful brick and tile battalion size units. All companies would spend their initial three weeks in the old barracks, then move to the new camps for their forth week (service week) and remain there throughout the remainder of their training period. It wasn't intended this way, to see the difference in young men's attitudes toward two opposite environments, but it happened within every company. Cadillac Sam had recently departed Great Lakes with a dishonorable discharge and the lectures requiring signatures, saying you would not take tea from the recruits, were almost a daily occurrence. Cadillac Sam got his name as a company commander from the fact he bought a new Cadillac each year. As a result he had come under investigation in the third year of pushing recruits and this revealed some interesting money making tactics or as we called it "tea taking." Sam presented his company with the utility bills like clock work each month. Always prompt and without delay each recruit in Sam's company must pay his share of the water, electricity, gas and sewage bill. According to Sam, it cost the government too much to house recruits in the first place and he would encourage them to conserve, but the bills they paid were always high. His recruits knew some others who were in another company, but as far as they knew their company commander was footing the bill so they wouldn't discuss something which wasn't their business. In basic training the total extent of a recruit's business is nothing.

Known names got around fast and you picked them up clear because these are the people you could be competing for company achievement awards, which incidently were transformed into your quarterly evaluation. Such nice names like, Charles the Head, Moore the Brain and Gleason the Cheat, made your job sound honest, decent and challenging to say the least.

Shortly after a brief training session, I was sent to Camp Berry to pick up my first company. I stood facing 140 young men in a large drill hall and when introduced over the speaker, several of them yawned, but kept quiet. Their beady little eyes told me they had been traveling all night and from their appearance and civilian dress, I could tell they had come from 140 different walks of life. I watched them curiously as they filed into the front door of the barber shop and tried to pick out the same one at the exit, but I could not determine the identity. The bully with the long hair, looked the same as Meek the Mouse and viceversa, when they came out the exit door. It was like robbing Sampson of his power by removing his hair. I would lose some of these young men during processing the first day, they would be held over for reasons like, bad teeth, can't read nor write, wet the bed, grabs other recruits privates, improper proof of citizenship and makes remarks to processing personnel. My first chance to talk with them came at around 10 p.m. on the second day and my primary mission was to calm them and create reassurance. The third day would be one of the most important and these individual results of test would follow them to their graves. For the first time they would meet someone different from those of the past two days and they would accept me as their one and only guardian, protector, counselor, and leader throughout the next eleven weeks. The beauty of it all blended in when I told them to stand at ease and come join me around the large wooden table. Their approach was almost like trying to make friends with the great African apes. A few cigarettes, permission to smoke and a lot of gentle words brought a flurry of questions ranging from,"Where are you from sir?" to,"What's going to happen to us sir?" Unknowing to these young men, this would be the one and only friend to friend conversation ever to be conducted with this company commander. The remainder of our meetings throughout this basic training would be prompt and strict.

The following afternoon I herded 92 of the original 140 men down the street from Camp Berry and moved the company into Camp Moffat. I could feel the battalion commander's eyes upon us as the company straggled along the road. Some of the men's peacoat sleeves were six inches beyond their hands and most all of the new issue trousers drag the ground behind them. I almost felt ashamed, but I knew they were my sole responsibility and I would lay down my life to protect each one.

Our first scheduled event for my company was to be on their first day after arrival at Camp Moffat. I teamed them together in mass stenciling, washing, rinsing, drying and folding of their entire clothing issued during the next two days. The weather held and we started the final phase of folding and storing their clothes by end of the second day. One young man named Ingram, was giving me a bit of trouble of several sorts. He was the shortest man in the company, came from Bloomfield, N.J. and could not say "sir", he had "Huh" stuck deep on his brain and I knew I would have to improve his attitude. All others were attentive and grasping knowledge fast, but Ingram was stubborn and figured everyone was picking on him.

Early on the third day we set out for our scheduled event to receive leggings and rifles. The rifles weighed eleven and one half pounds and once received, it would be known to the recruit as his piece. I had instructed the company to return themselves to the exact spot after issue and stand with the piece in front of their chests, barrel to their left and keep their mouth shut. Watching through the window, I observed Ingram returning to the last position in the second platoon and the rifle was actually longer than he was tall. He wanted to discuss the size of this thing with some of the other recruits returning to position but they ignored him and followed my instructions because they were smart enough to know I was watching from inside. As soon as the last man had assembled, I walked out of the building and yelled,"Ingram, hit the deck!" He dropped immediately and commenced, "One sir, two sir, three sir." I commanded the company to "Forward March" and left him on the ground. He knew he couldn't get up until he was ordered to do so, and I knew the man inside the building would see him out there and since he didn't have anything else to do, he would have him some fun with Ingram. I took the company to a drill field about one quarter mile from the building and commenced teaching them how to carry the piece without poking each others eyes out. They would be taught to use it for saluting, challenging, drilling, perform the sixteen count manual, then ultimately the ninety six count manual, all within seventy two hours. After about forty five minutes, I heard what sounded like a horse running down the road and looked to see Ingram coming. He had his rifle hoisted above his head and was screaming out to me,"Sir, Sir, please take me back." I stepped off the drill platform and met him. I'll never forget his words or the pleading in his voice when he said,"Sir, please take me back, I promise to never say huh again as long as I live." His eyes were pale and crying, and I knew his strength was gone. All the buttons were missing from the front of his shirt and the man at the building had made him eat them. Both ends of his shirt collar had been chewed off and swallowed and his shoe lacing was missing. He was soaking wet from the top of his head to his toe nails and had fine coal dust all over his body. I placed my hand on his shoulder and led him into his position at the rear of the second platoon. Within minutes of this incident, I could feel and see the spark of a brilliant company of men coming together now as one great force. I knew that day as we returned to the barracks, by the sharpness, the zest and determination of these young men, this would be a hard company to bring down.

The next two weeks were like wild fire on schedule from four a.m. till six p.m. daily, schooling, drilling, inspection, studying, washing and folding clothing and personal hygiene. Ingram had been appointed as guidon for Company 473 and was carrying the company flag with the greatest of pride. I had selected my R.P.O.C. (Recruit Petty Officer Chief) in a young man from Rochester, N.Y. My selection of Master-at-Arms, Platoon Leaders, Squad Leaders, Mail Petty Officer and Religious Petty Officer, had been completed and finalized. Company 473 was primarily made up of small young men and they were sharp and quick in maneuvers. They were especially clean and some had been rather taken aback by the old barracks. Their minds were keen and they grasped instructions on the first go-around. The majority of these young men came from the Northern U.S. and forty- two were from the Rochester, N.Y. area alone. When asked, I always told them I came from a cotton farm just south of Syracuse, N.Y. The recruits would grin at this remark, but never persist or challenge my truthfulness.

On Monday of the third week Company 473 was issued the Second Battalion Drill Flag and Star Flag (cleanliness) and by the end of that week, they had won the right to carry the Second Regiment Drill and Star Flags. These are the highest awards achievable within the first three weeks. By this time Charles the Head, Moore the Brain and Gleason the Cheat, knew Company 473 and their company commander were out there. Charles and Moore were up ahead with Companies 451 and 463 respectively and I was getting feed back from the First Regiment. Gleason had picked up behind me and was trying to organize Company 486, but was stuck with an experimental bed wetter. The Navy was attempting to rehabilitate these young men with the problem and I had just escaped under the wire. Gleason had been issued a rubber mattress, but couldn't resolve nor get from under the problem, so his Star Award capabilities weren't a threat to me at the time. Charles and Moore were coming off service week, just as I would be going on, so they would be locking horns together until I arrived in the First Regiment. Charles' bag was the Drill Flags and he usually kept these locked in. On the other hand Moore's real interest lay in the Star Flags and he locked those in. The "I" Intelligent Flags and "A" Athletic Flags fell in a general competition scheme with both men. Gleason had no particular interest in any award in general and would cheat every way possible to keep a competitive company from earning those flags.

The company's fourth week was service week and they would be assigned to every make of chore within the First and Second Regiments. Some would mess cook, while others mowed grass, stood gate guard, assisted dental and medical, dug ditches, shoveled coal and what have you. It was time for me to rest and prepare for the competition of training schedules ahead, but I couldn't rest and kept a weary eye on my men. Some jobs were clean, but the recruits assigned dirty jobs got dirty and I needed to constantly prod them or they would surely never catch up in the few hours allowed before fifth week competition. There wouldn't have been any chance to rest anyway, because too many things are happening all the time. I was called to the clinic about an incident with one of my recruits, which had resulted in a five year veteran medic being placed on report by the doctor. As it happened, my recruit had come there for sick call and listed his complaint as blisters. With recruits wearing new oversized shoes, it would be one out of a thousand chances the recruit would have blisters anyplace other than on the heels of his feet. When the medic ordered all blister complaints to remove shoes and socks then place their nose against the wall, naturally each young man obeyed. When he examined my recruits heels, he ran him out of the clinic and accused him of fluffing from his work. The recruit returned and made out the second complaint and again ended up in the line up. This time the medic got rough and shoved him to the floor and may have kicked him. A doctor had seen this and placed the medic on report, while the medic was accusing the recruit of shirking duty and lying about having blisters. As I talked with my recruit, he showed me both hands and the large blisters had broken. Both hands were bleeding and it was partially caused by the medic shoving him face down into the hard floor. This recruit had been pushing a manual grass cutter for two days and someone in the regiment had neglected to issue him gloves. He was finally treated and bandaged and I took him to regiment and got his classification changed to clerk for the remainder of the service week. Since I was still officially attached to the Second Regiment Company Commander Staff, I was ordered to sit in on a Second Regiment Review of a case involving Gleason and Company 486. Gleason had come under investigation for mistreating recruits and all company commanders would hear the case and beware. It all started in Gleason's first week of training for Company 486, when Gleason spoke out of turn at a battalion meeting and demanded the battalion commander do something about that bed wetter assigned to his company. The following day Gleason's company failed barracks inspection, but it wasn't the bed wetter who caused the failure. Another recruit had left a bundle of clothes stops (small lines used for tying clothes on the line for drying) tucked under his mattress. Apparently, when Gleason learned of this he went to the class room where the recruit was attending scheduled classes and removed the young man back to his barracks. Inside each company living space, the company commander keeps two recruits on guard at all times who are rotated every two hours and are excused from all other duties while on post. Gleason ordered the two recruit guards to hold the young man's feet and placed him out the second story window. Gleason hung his head out the window and was telling the recruit of certain agreements he must vow to or he would order the guards to drop him. Gleason didn't see the Pepsi-Cola truck, which was traveling below and servicing the barracks Pepsi machines, but the driver saw the recruit and as he pointed to show his helper, the trucks right front wheel hit the curb and bounced off the road into a large dumpster. At the sound of a crash outside, Gleason ordered the guards to lift the recruit and swiftly return to their post. He ordered the recruit to return to the classroom on the double and when the security police, fire truck and regimental commander arrived, Gleason denied and the two recruit guards swore there had been no unusual happenings in the barracks. The Pepsi truck driver and helper are probably still wondering today what or who it was they saw, but the regimental commander knew Gleason and wasn't to be taken far off into left field about this. He told Gleason to report to his office that afternoon and when he arrived he asked Gleason how the bed wetter was doing. Gleason said he didn't have anymore problems with the bed wetter, but wouldn't tell the commander how he had resolved the problem. He again denied anything unusual happening in his barracks that morning. That night the regimental commander returned to Camp Moffat and went to Gleason's company about 11 p.m. Mandatory bed times for recruits is 9 p.m. and most always the company commander will be gone shortly afterwards. The regimental commander ordered the lights be turned on and conducted a bed check. He found the bed wetter was missing and the recruit guards would not tell where he was. Further inspection of the company area found the recruit asleep in a long urinal trough. Gleason apparently decided this young lad could wet during the night to his hearts content and this was the ideal spot. Gleason received a general court martial the following week as I was digging in to compete for my company's fifth week and he received a dishonorable discharge.

My company was in trouble the first of their fifth week but, within two days they began to roll. I blamed lots of the problems on their move from an old to a new barracks, but what was really happening was, the young men were now realizing and finding each others faults. Some friction developed as a result and my R.P.O.C. and M.A.A. had placed seven recruits on report. This meant I would have to trial, jury and judge these men as quickly as possible. I stayed over that night and held mast on each one separately. Punishment was harsh and fast, so when it was over, I told my R.P.O.C. and M.A.A., who sat in on each case, if I had a dollar, I'd go get a beer. The M.A.A. shot out of my office and returned shortly with a white hat full of bills. I reached into the hat and crumpled a few in my hand, put on my hat and left. I knew I needed to give them some time to sort things out alone and really I needed to sort my mind out a bit, too. When I arrived at the Company Commanders Club, all the heavy hitters were there. I would guess, that over the years, more than a million Hall of Fame companies have been pushed over that bar. Shortly after my arrival, the two base Chaplains came in. One Catholic, the other Protestant and they wanted to play for some money, so I checked to see what I had in the crumpled pile. I counted $36.00, so I played and won and left one hour later with $82.00.

Early the next morning, I was summoned to the First Regiment Office and told the base executive officer wanted to see me in his office on main side. When I arrived, his clerk brought me coffee and the "XO" asked how my company was coming along. He said he had heard of them in competition and wished me well, but he was concerned about one of my recruits named Sepe. Quickly it flashed through my mind, Sepe was one of the small cases held in my office last night. The "XO" continued, and told me of the commanding officer of Recruit Training receiving a letter which indicated I had a full Navy captain in training within my company. He said the C.O. was somewhat concerned about this and wanted such doings put to an end. Apparently, Sepe had written his parents and told them he had been promoted to captain and his parents had told an ex-army Sergeant, Sepe's uncle, about this. He knew better and the parents had questioned our commanding officer about this by mail. I told the "XO" I'd take care of the matter and returned to Camp Dewey to shift my company for scheduled classes. At days end, I sent for Sepe and told my R.P.O.C. and M.A.A. to remain in my office. When Sepe arrived, he stood at attention in front of my desk as I told the R.P.O.C. to dictate my words for an entry into Sepe's permanent service jacket. I asked Sepe where he was from and he said,"Cleveland, Ohio, Sir." I told him he was about to make history and so was I. Then I told the R.P.O.C. to take note: Let it be known by all men present, that on this day, March 3rd, 1964, as Chief Petty Officer, United States Navy and Company Commander of Recruit Company 473, use the powers vested in me to reduce United States Navy Captain, Mr. Sepe, to seaman recruit in the United States Navy. I told Sepe,"you have now involved me in history to be the first chief ever, and there will never be one again to break a captain to recruit". He was ordered to get a pen, pad and envelope by the M.A.A. and when Sepe returned to the office, he wrote his parents the truth for a change. I read the letter aloud and sealed it for mailing personally the following morning. No problem came of Sepe or any of the other recruits along these lines again.

Company 473 had gotten through the fifth week with good grades overall, but not good enough, so I spent the day Sunday with them preparing for what we must do. They had taken the swim, rope climb, and relay events on Saturday, but we needed all four events in order to compete for the "A" flag. Our hardest and the one we were losing was the tug-of-war. All company rope pullers were huge, but I didn't have any huge men in Company 473. I'd have to think about this one and I knew somehow there was a way. Charles was still up ahead with Drill locked in and Moore was out there with the Star locked up. I had another problem trying to figure out how to get the Brigade "I" which would pass me by in the next two weeks if I didn't find a solution. I had to get away from the recruits and do some thinking. Realizing they could not reach the level of achievement I desired on their own, I knew I must pull some tricks out of the hat. I stopped by the pool where my daughter was taking diving lessons and relaxed, watching the pretty young girls dive from the board. As one of the girls did a twist in mid air from the diving board, my mind snapped and it was something I knew all along. The body will go anywhere the eyes go and the head is the heaviest portion. That was it and I knew a way to win the tug-of-war event.

When I arrived home I had visitors from Detroit, an old Navy buddy and his wife were being transferred there for duty and stopped by to say hello. We discussed my company's problems and in the discussion of the intelligent achievement, he told me he might be able to help. A good friend of his worked in the Clerical Office and had access to the recruits' final exams. He told me he would check into this and get back to me later, then they left.

By the end of the day, on Monday of the sixth week in training, Company 473 had edged to within 8 points of Moore's Company 463. They were putting everything they had into these inspections and would no doubt take the battalion that week. I had picked my tug-of-war team carefully and didn't necessarily select some of the bigger men. I needed determination and loyalty, rather than weight in the team. I beefed up the swim, rope climb and relay teams for a sure thing and I would attend the tug-of-war events. On Wednesday night my old buddy brought me three series of recruit final exams. For these, his friend needed $100.00 in cash and I gladly paid. I knew there was no way I could chance copying or handing this material to my recruits, so I taped these tests throughout the night. The next day I was called to regiment and told all companies starting with Company 450 were being reduced to nine weeks training instead of eleven. This placed Company 451 and Company 463 into my graduating grouping and really made the cheese binding for me to catch up from behind. I decided to start the exam tapes on Thursday night and play them continuously through each night until the final exams came in on the eighth week.

By the end of the sixth week, Company 473 had taken the Battalion Star, Drill and Intelligent flags. Needless to say they were going to be hard to hold back now, and on Saturday they would compete for the Battalion "A". On Saturday morning the company's athletic teams mustered in at the four events, which were located in different areas of the base, as if each came to slaughter the other. I held last minute briefings with my tug-of-war team and told each of them to lay back gently on the rope, select a board on the top of the Drill Hall with their eyes and when the man yelled pull, walk back towards that board. Under no circumstances was any man to raise his head during the event. When their company number was called for the first pull, they calmly picked up the rope and got a good grip. Their spacing was good and when the man said "Ready" they lay straight back head low and set their feet. Then suddenly came the yell, "Pull". I heard the rope pop and eight big blundering recruits came sailing over the line. The event was halted and they looked toward me and smiled. The other company was bewildered, because the small group shouldn't have been able to drag that much weight over the line, much less pull weight and strength over. Time and time again that day word reached me of wins for my company in swims, rope climbs, relay races and I was watching the tug-of-war team take every event. At the end of that day, I received word from the regiment my company hadn't stopped at battalion or regiment level, but had won the Brigade "A" flag. I thought at this time the company could possibly make the Hall of Fame and to do this, they only needed the other three brigade awards which were,"Star", "I", and "Drill". During their preparations on Sunday for the drill competition, I felt sure they could beat Charles' Company 451 in the seventh week if I gave them a boost. So on Tuesday of their seventh week they received the scheduled event. When they assembled on the grinder, prior to marching to the Drill Hall, I asked them to gather around me. I told them some jokes and at the same time permitted those who desired to have a smoke. They calmed down and gained confidence and as they fell back into ranks, I placed one jelly bean in each recruit's mouth. When they were commanded to right shoulder arms for moving out, the brisk snap of every move was perfectly precise. Enroute to the Drill Hall, I noticed a sub-contractor replacing shingles on top of one of the half moon shaped roofs. A workman on top of the building was making mouse ears at the company and this irritated me, since it might de-motivate the company toward their very important event. By now, Company 473 had acquainted themselves so well with my voice until they could make precision moves at a whisper. So in a low voice I said "company halt, order arms, right face, (facing the men on the roof) firing position, take aim" and at that the roofers ran over the roof and some of them accidently slid off the other side and fell 28 feet to the ground. I put my company back in marching formation and continued toward the Drill Hall as the recruits grinned and looked straight ahead. The incident was reported to Regiment, but the roofers couldn't identify the company number or the company commander. When we arrived at the Drill Hall, our precise positioning and swift countdown made Charles nervous. Naturally when the company commander gets upset, the recruits know it and they always follow suit. They know every expression of their company commander's and know what each indicates. Some company commanders may have a limp when he walks and after the third week, you can recognize his recruits by that limp. Needless to say, I gave them a big smile as they completed the competitive exercise that morning, because Charles could never pull himself or his troops back together. Now it was two down and two to go and they had beat out the heavies and they very well knew it. The tapes rattled on every night during their sleep with questions and answers to every test the recruits would be subjected to. I knew they would only take one of the three series, but didn't know which one, so they were getting the full coarse. Now that Company 473 had put Charles down with Company 451, our main obstacle was Moore, with Company 463, and the Brigade "Star". No one stood in out way for the Brigade "I" and it hadn't been carried by any company for six months. The tapes would have to take their course for the "I" flag and there was nothing else I could do about that. Moore had 16th battalion commander duty on Saturday night and caught my one of my recruits returning from the snack bar with a pocket full of Slim Jims. Some of the recruits in my company had sent money by him and he was returning 38 Slim Jims to the barracks. My R.P.O.C. told me about the event upon my arrival Sunday morning, to assume my duty as battalion commander of the 14th battalion for that day. Moore had questioned the recruit about the company functions and had made him drink a cup of hot black coffee while he watched him eat the 38 Slim Jims, one by one at Moore's command. My only purpose in life that day was to retaliate against Moore, other than carry out my assigned duties as battalion commander. The first thing I did was catch one of his recruits not double timing while traveling in single formation and since he had wings in his white hat, I assigned him to taxi an R-5-D aircraft up and down the side walk for three hours (simulated). I caught another passing the 14th battalion office with his peacoat unbuttoned and when I attempted to pull one of the buttons off for him to eat, the entire front of the coat ripped away exposing the lining. I realized these knuckleheads had sewn their peacoat buttons on with copper wire, I went to the clothing store and bought another peacoat to keep myself out of trouble. When I drove back from dinner that night one of Moore's recruits had been placed on duty as road guard to the 14th battalion grinder. That was where I parked my car, but now I was being challenged by this recruit. He told me his duties and he could not let me pass through his post. I told him to get out of the way or I'd run over him and proceeded to the parking area. Since this post came under the 14th battalion jurisdiction, the recruit reported the violation to me at the end of his watch. When he knocked loudly on the battalion office door, I told him to enter. He stepped swiftly into the office, a precise three step forward, turned right, popped to attention and saluted. At the same time, holding his salute he started, "Sir, I wish to report a violation of my post, sir". A recruit must salute anything that moves and must hold his salute until he receives a return or is directed to carry on. Since I wasn't covered (wearing my hat) at the time, I just sat staring into the recruits eyes. I told him to go outside and try again. Forty five minutes later and after his twenty fifth entry, I told him to drop his salute and report. He held a small note in one hand and stated, "Sir, a violation of my post occurred at 18:30 this date. One commander driving a blue 1959 Ford, Illinois License D-16501L, passed through my post." I asked the recruit what he thought we should do about this terrible thing and he stated, "Sir, I wish to eat this paper so as to assure myself there never was a violation of my post." I told him he had my permission and after he had swallowed the paper, I told him to get out of my office and never let me see him again. At that he left and like lightening he was gone.

On Monday of the 8th week, I talked with my R.P.O.C. and told him the feud between Mr. Moore's recruits and mine must stop. We discussed our possibilities to achieve the Intelligence award at the end of that week and if so, we would saboteur Mr. Moore's barracks inspection. We knew our recruits must watch for the same tactics and they would be instructed not to deviate from any current policy as a result of conversation with any recruits outside of Company 473. Some of the things that could happen were underlined for special attention. These things could range from a rumor of change at the diner during meals, to stragglers falling in at the rear of our company's formation causing us to receive road demerits. Anything happening now could knock Company 473 out of a chance to achieve Hall of Fame.

On Friday evening, I was called to regiment and

congratulated upon receipt of the bright new white flag, with a large red "I" in the center. Company 473 had won the Brigade "I" award from the final exam results taken on Wednesday. This was the first issue of the Brigade "I" in over six months. The following day the company achieved their Second Brigade "A" award for overall team athletic wins and only one award was left to worry about. I called my R.P.O.C. in and told him to select a highly convincing recruit for a special mission. He sent me a recruit named Flowers, who hailed from High Point, N.C. Flowers had lied to me on several occasions during the training cycle, but had always convinced me that he was telling the truth, so I knew the R.P.O.C. had chosen his man well. I told Flowers he would slip a secret to Mr. Moore's company clerk at dinner. He was only to tell him the hem tuck was no longer required on the recruit jersey, effective Monday. There were two elements involved in my theory of approach and I believed it would work without repercussions. The wool turtle neck jersey had become a mandatory part of the recruit clothing issue in January, that year. Since its existence, the folding and storage problems of wool and the instructions had been a sore topic for all company commanders. Once they had it stowed properly in the recruits locker, they never allowed him to touch it again. Therefore, when the company commander made his routine locker check, usually just prior to afternoon inspection, he didn't bother to look over the jersey's storage. Another thing was when a recruit hears of a change to regulations from recruits outside his jurisdiction he readily accepts this as fact and will act quickly, especially if its something his company commander isn't aware of. This allows the recruit to save the day and get a pat on the back. Since recruit inspection of their personal hygiene habits during training is maintained on a 24 hour basis, all recruits will attempt to assist each other with helpful hints. Their communicating techniques are unique and probably 90% of this informal correspondence and verbal leads are never known by their individual company commanders. The inspection process starts with all recruits on the line for personnel inspection at 6 a.m. every day during training. He is inspected by a brigade inspector for cleanliness, shave, uniform dress and posture. If any recruit fails a portion of the inspection, points will be deducted from the company competitive scores for that week. If all the recruits in one company or a majority have the same discrepancy, regardless of type of inspection, the company will receive a 000 (triple out) for the event and probably be knocked out of any chance to compete during that week. Point system is based on a perfect 4.00 and the inspection sub-standard level occurs when a company reaches 2.50 for any single inspection or for a weekly average. During each morning, except Sundays, the recruit is delivered to scheduled classes or drills by his company commander and no one is allowed to return to the barracks. It is at this time when the brigade inspector conducts a rigid inspection of the recruits living quarters, wash room, bath rooms, and clothes lines, even the company commanders office is affected by the system. Everything must be stowed and cleaned to a specific individual regulation. The recruits may be allowed to return at noon, time permitting, but must not touch or move anything within the barracks. The afternoon inspection is specifically for locker storage, clothes storage, cleanliness of stowed items and uniformity, but may also recap the morning inspection, if the barracks have been used. Again the point system prevails and all three inspections' results are totaled out for a one day company average. End of the week figures are total weekly inspection averages and with Company 463 carrying a 3.92 weekly average, it would be hard for Company 473 to win out with maximum individual inspection of 3.86. Thus, the meaningful thing to do would be to start Mr. Moore off early in the week with a triple 000.

Company 473 was in classes on Monday afternoon when the axe fell in the 16th battalion and it was like a bomb exploded down there. Moore knew what had happened, but he couldn't prove anything, because the clerk didn't know what company the other recruit was in. I would make sure the clerk never identified him, even if it meant bringing his food and leaving him on watch when the company was moving. Moore filed a complaint of ethics with the regimental commander, but that didn't stop the weekly figures from reaching the computer and Company 473 taking the Brigade Star Flag on Friday. Companies 450 through 490 would graduate on the following Tuesday, which was their ninth week and I would have to say bye to each of my men on Wednesday and Thursday. I had not received any official confirmation as to Company 473 being selected to the Hall of Fame and as minutes went by I knew I had missed something in my planning. I took out all my records and tallied up the company awards. They had achieved six Battalion Stars, three Regimental Stars and one Brigade Star. Also one Regimental "I", one Brigade "I", and one Regimental Drill, two Brigade Drills, three Battalion "A"s , two Regimental "A"s and two Brigade "A"s. I totaled up twenty two awards and a company needs only twelve specifically placed awards to be considered for entry into Hall of Fame, at least that's the way I understood the rules.

On Monday of the company's ninth week I went to regiment and questioned them about my company's standings and was told to my disbelief, that my company had failed to achieve one award of which we had all agreed was the most important achievement of all. Company 473 had failed to earn the right to carry and display the flag of the United States of America at their graduation ceremony. In my fight to win against the big guns I had neglected to carry a constant average. For example, once my company was credited for the highest award within that event, I dropped that ball and went after another. Back behind me was Company 481, which was commanded by a man named Nelson and I'd never heard of the company nor of the man mentioned in competition. While I was up front knocking all the big guns out of the way, he was drifting smoothly along with the overall highest recruit average, and although he did not win any of the recruit flags, his company won the right to graduate as color company by beating my company out. We had lost by 3 overall training average points for the nine week period. It took a while for this to soak in and it even looked very weird at graduation ceremonies when Nelson's Company 481 marched out ahead of my Company 473. His company only displayed two guidons, one carrying the company flag and one carrying our Stars and Stripes. Company 473 was second in passing review and their front lines displayed the company flag guidon, and twelve achievement awards guidons with pendants indicating the twenty two awards. I observed a visiting Japanese Navy Admiral pointing and then asking our commanding officer, "What gives here?" I had worked so hard with this company and been away from my home so many hours these past nine weeks, that my wife refused to even consider attending the ceremony, and I felt kind of like the admiral, "What gives here?"

I spent the next two days bidding farewell to all my men and for the first time revealed to them I wasn't from a cotton farm outside Syracuse, N.Y., but instead came from a farm in Madison County, Ga. To tell them wasn't necessary because they already knew. I was removed from training recruits and assigned as instructor to prospective company commanders for the next three years at Great Lakes. This was a newly programmed training procedure and I enjoyed it, for the most it took the first recruit company sub-standard grades and educated all company commanders to an equal and uniform training capability, thus eliminating the commander's first company being sent to the fleet with less opportunity of achievement than his second or third company.

Six years passed without seeing any of the recruits or now young sailors, whom I had commanded at Great Lakes and when I met Ingram at Charleston in 1970, it was an honored get together. He told me one of the soundest memories of all was the taped final exams. He readily repeated four questions and answers to the exam and said he remembers many more even after six years had passed.

If I were to dedicate this true story, it would be to

two of the finest, honest and dedicated Naval officers I met during my naval career. To my commanding officer and to my executive officer, I owe my most sincere appreciation for my tour of duty at Great Lakes, Ill.

"THE BET"

The welfare and recreation fund committee on board the U.S.S. Hunley AS-31 was about the tightest organization with coins that I've ever known. Sometimes they would spring for a couple of soft balls after the others in use became balls of string when you attempted to catch a fly ball. To get money out of the fund was like trying to get a bank loan while unemployed with no collateral. So its no wonder how surprised we were one day when the recreation committee issued a notice to sponsor 50% of the cost for a deep sea fishing trip. To charter a boat with enough fishing space to accommodate those desiring to go in two separate groups would cost $14.00 per person and the fund would support $7.00 each. Everyone was permitted to bring one guest at the same cost, but the guest must be a wife, girlfriend or child over 18 years old and would be responsible directly to the sponsor.

Stationed on board the Hunly was a big, fat chief cook, who managed to call off for business on shore each time the ship got underway to make short trips out to sea for classified reasons. He was unusually excited about this trip to the Blackfish banks and boasted of the fish he would catch to the extent I got irritated with him. I had gotten tired of hearing his big mouth so I told him he would never fish because he would be sea sick. He got mad about my attitude and said he'd bet me $50.00 he wouldn't and on top of that, he'd bet me another $50.00 he'd catch more fish than I did. I'd already run my mouth like a fool. I bet him he would get sick but wouldn't take him up on the catch bet. The more I thought about it the worse I felt because I couldn't afford to loose a fifty and didn't know where I'd get it if I lost. I couldn't back out though, because he had told everyone by now about the bet and it was I who started this mess. I knew he would have a tough time anyway, because he didn't have any sea time and was heavy with fluid. However with all this confidence which he was building up made me figure I had best get an ace up my sleeve in case the jetties and sea motion didn't get him. I searched my brain for several days for a fool proof scheme and a few days before the trip one snapped into my mind. I thought it out real good and set a pattern of sequence, almost as practicing for a stage show and when I thought about it I broke into a grin because I could use the extra fifty. He continued to prepare himself with confidence right up to the day before our trip but I never doubted that my plan wouldn't work.

The night before our trip was to begin at 6 a.m. the following day, I took one stiff strand of spaghetti from the box at home and placed it into a pan of warm water. I let it set over night and the next morning it was much larger in diameter and very flexible. I wrapped it in a napkin and placed it inside my coat pocket where it would stay moist and warm. When I met the chief at the boat landing he asked if I wanted to chicken out on our bet. He said he'd give me one last chance to save my money and I told him I'd take my chances. As the boat left the dock he stuck very close to me and watched my every move. It was still dark and chilly so most everyone went below and sat on the five long benches which ran from forward to aft on the boat. I knew this could be a bad mistake for them since the benches were located right over the big diesel engines and these fumes along with the noise could cause sickness. I couldn't talk the chief into going below unless I went with him and I sure wasn't taking a chance so we stood on the stern and talked. The river was smooth, but as we approached the mouth we began to encounter ground swells. On both sides of the boat you could see the large jetties jutting up into the morning dawn and it seemed like the seas would be smooth that day. There were no clouds in the sky and the wind was dead calm so I was beginning to worry when suddenly the chief stretched his arms upwards and taking a deep breath, he said, "Ummm, get a load of this good fresh sea air." At that time I noticed he was slightly white around the lips and under the eyes, also he had begun to swallow rapidly. I knew the ground swells had done a good job but soon we would be in smooth seas and he might recover so I decided to make my move. I told him I had to go to the rest room, the one place only one person could get into at a time, so he couldn't follow me. He said o.k. and I stepped down the short ladder and opened the door to the cabin. Many of the people who were sitting when we left the dock were now laying on the benches. It was very warm in there and those who were sitting up didn't look very good at all. The rest room was just inside the cabin door to my right so I stepped inside and locked the door. I took out the flexible length of spaghetti and packed about one inch of it in my nose. I placed the other end of it in my mouth. As I left the rest room, I covered my face with my hand but when I left the cabin door I removed my hand and put my foot on the bottom step of the short ladder. I was stopped there suddenly facing two women who had been on deck and were returning to the cabin. They were pale like ghost and staring at my face. I tried to cover my nose and mouth but it was too late. They both ran to the starboard side of the boat, upchucking as they went. When they reached the lifeline the wind caught their spray and it went flying aft into the chief, who had walked over to the lifeline in my absence. He turned in the morning dawn as if startled at first, then with their upchuck in his face, he joined them. I ran to the port side and threw the spaghetti overboard. Sickness spread thoughout the boat rapidly as if there was an epidemic and very little fishing was done during the day. People would come out and try, but just couldn't hold out, so they would return to their bucket and call for O'Rouke. I stood on the stern and caught black bass like they were going out of style and the boat captain came back to talk with me around 2:30 p.m. He said, "To be a bunch of sailors, this is the sickest group I've ever carried out." He asked me if I saw anything unusual happen early this morning and I told him I didn't. Since I had more fish than I could carry, he said he was going on back into port because he was afraid these people might not recover right away even with their feet on solid ground. I told him I was ready and when we got back that day I had to drag two large sacks full of fish off the pier. It was a good thing I caught the fish, because the chief never did pay me the fifty.

"LAST CRUISE"

When we consider the characteristics of a sea going vessel regardless of its shape or size, we must never take self containment for granted. To all men of the high seas their ship is regarded by landlubbers with utmost respect and pride. Terms commonly heard from sailors are, she is a great ship, or she has some problems with her engines. This response is a direct refection of the love and care received from ones mother. Even ships steaming in a fleet of flotilla will have one which is referred to as the mother ship, when they are of the same class they will be known as sister ships. Never has one been referred to as father or brother and this reflects the sincere devotion and love for his women, wherever she may be. The ship is self contained and must furnish the necessities of survival for each member of her crew. Environmental standards and codes of conduct must be strictly obeyed through self discipline. She has been designed to provide for, and perform her every duty, within the realm of her children's capabilities, attitudes and obedience.

When reporting on board a different ship for duty a sailor is normally reluctant and wary at first. This comes from the love of his last home. Usually this is in the form of constructive criticism, since he must bear in mind any ship is only as good as the men who live within her hull. With this in mind most all men will strive to make their ship better within a short time of reporting and freely offer suggestions of new ways in special care which he may have used to improve his last ship. In any case, this is his living limits within the distance he can travel up or down, side to side or from end to end, unless he has brought along some special sort of shoes which would allow him to get off and walk back home. A ships age, temperament, troubles, problems and capabilities are discussed by seamen from all areas of the continent and may be often nicknamed, killer, pot belly, super star, jinxes or many others, but her underlying reputation is always reflective of the current crew or crews which she has previously carried.

One such was a very old L.S.T. (Landing Ship Transport) which I reported aboard at Charleston, South Carolina. My very first impression was to know where the life jackets were stowed and how to exit in a hurry. She had a newly assigned captain who was a congenial man. His very first desire was to have a happy and contented crew. He roamed freely among the crew collecting their gripes and pet peeves and to say the least they had plenty. This ship had orders to put to sea within a few days after my reporting and I think most of the crew would rather stay behind and go fishing. Their attitudes as a whole were very poor and a good percentage were totally apathetic toward the upcoming cruise. On board was one chief boatswain mate and he completely disagreed with the captain's concerns about the crew and maintained the ship's care and crews discipline was of most importance. I didn't like him in particular but agreed with him in principal. Our ship was no doubt in bad shape and we needed to get together as a team and correct many situations to make her sea worthy. I pointed out areas which were in desperate need of maintenance or repair, but no one seemed interested in helping, so I did the best I could to prepare the ship for sailing. Taking short cuts or jury rigging wasn't my nature and I knew these methods eventually would fail, but I didn't have much time to work with. Our duties during this trip would be to furnish logistic support to a squadron of wooden hull mine sweepers and their supplies seemed to come second to the crew's needs. Nevertheless we set sail on time and all things seemed to be in order. I figured when we got out of the Ashley River mouth and into open sea we would start making some speed on our first leg of the trip, which was to Roosevelt Roads, Porta Rica. I was sort of surprised to find out we had been running at the ships flank speed while coming down the river and that was all of 8 knots (11.2 m.p.h.) Even in calm seas this was going to be one long, long trip. If you can imagine how long it took you to get some place in a straight line, traveling at flank speed you can readily realize how long it would take you to get back, even if you turned around now. The mine sweepers were considerably faster than my ship so they went off to play war games and would join up with us each night and travel in formation during the dark hours. After all, we were their mother ship and their total dependance was focused on us. The first day out of Charleston we lost bilge suction and our after steering room began flooding. A quick check of the piping revealed I could crush each suction line with my hand like a Dixie cup so I resorted to the only emergency repair I knew and that was the fiber glass repair kits we carried for damage control purposes. Line after line located in the ships bilges broke during the afternoon due to vibration coming from the propeller and I worked feverishly to keep the ship from flooding. At dusk on the first day I came topside and onto the main deck to get some fresh air and when I looked toward the ships stern, I could still see land on the horizon. We definitely hadn't gone many miles but when you travel at a steady slow speed, 24 hours each day, you will travel further than you think. Most of the next seven days and nights were about the same as the first, with constant leaks and problems in long overdue maintenance areas. We had to take on fuel while underway and almost collided with the tanker several times, twice we had to cut away and once the tanker broke away from us. Our ship's speed combined with its flat bottom caused us to shift forty feet in any direction, at times without any rudder control whatsoever. Finally arriving in the bright blue waters of Puerto Rico, we anchored in about 100 feet of water and the mine sweepers set up their dummy mine fields and began playing hide and seek. The navy base at Roosevelt Roads sent a helicopter out to help the sweepers locate dummy mines and I admired the way it would travel rapidly along the water's surface with its nose almost touching. On the second day it stuck its nose too close and our landing craft had to go pick up the pilot and crew members from the water. They were safe and that was what really mattered. On the third day our evaporators went out and since we only had one we were immediately put on water hours. At first the water fountains remained on but you only had one hour per day to get a shower and wash up. Our landing craft took the pilot and crew member of the downed helicopter to the sandy beach to be picked up by jeep dispatched by the navy base and when he dropped the boat's ramp the coatswain didn't notice the sand which got between the ramp door and the boat. Upon his return the boats speed kept the ramp door above the water but when he stopped at the ship our landing craft sank in 120 feet of water. The coatswain and engineer floated out and climbed up the ship's side using Jacobs ladder. By now, the captain was beginning to harden and was showing some strain within his forced smile. The flooding, evaporators down, a helicopter along with our landing craft on the ocean bottom were the kind of happenings which were about to bring out the realization of the incompetence in a non-disciplined ship's crew. On the fifth day at anchor, two deep sea divers arrived from Trinidad and made a dive to find our boat. By now we had completely run out of fresh water and was drinking juices along with taking salt water showers. We didn't have any salt water soap on board and my hair was standing straight up along with many others who had used ordinary soaps for washing their hair. The divers located our boat and secured a floating buoy to it. They went back down on the sixth day guiding the rear section of our anchor cable to the boat. They saddled it with a large cable and we began lowering the huge beaching anchor slowly. As the boat reached about 10 feet depth it would come no further so the boatswain mate connected the boat loading crane to it. He succeeded in surfacing the top of the boat but burned out the motor in our winch. I began throwing every submersible pump we had on board into the boat and with all of them pumping, the boat began to surface slowly. By the time the boat floated we only had two of the six pumps left which would function. The following morning we hoisted anchor and towed our landing craft into San Juan, where the captain laid down the law to everyone, but it was too late to do much good. we stayed in port for seven days while a crew of technicians fixed our evaporators and on the last night a few major contributors were allowed to go ashore. I went with another sailor and about three minutes after the cab dropped us in old San Juan city, we were robbed at gun point. With no money, nor identification we returned to the ship but our story wasn't anything unusual about San Juan, so I went to bed. Early the next morning we left San Juan harbor and headed south. We had loaded fresh provisions and with our evaporators going again, it seemed that things might get better,but after only two hours out there was an explosion on our bow. The water was burning on one side of the ship and it looked like our main deck was on fire from the bow to almost mid ship. Our fire hoses swept the fire over the side and it was under control in about five minutes. One man was removed from the bow and carried below for treatment of sever burns and shock. He had been welding, replacing a rusted out lifeline stanchion when the explosion occurred. Investigation proved that one of two fifty gallon drums filled with gasoline and located on the bow was leaking and the gas had crept along the main deck to where the welder was working. I went to sick bay to visit the welder and noticed a five gallon glass container setting on a thin piece of plywood. I asked the medic what was in the jug and he told me it was 190 proof alcohol. I knew then why he stayed half crocked all the time, so I told my friends about it and we decided he didn't have a right to all that white liquor. That night I measured out the area from below and we drilled a small hole through the steel floor of sick bay. When the drill brought out wooden chips, I knew we had the right spot but the drill bit wouldn't penetrate the glass jug. We rigged a hose to the hole and placed a small steel rod through until it touched the bottom of the jub. One sharp tap on the rod and we had white lightening pouring all over the place and before it quit we had collected almost a quart through the small hole. We scampered across the tank deck and up the other side of the ship to our berthing compartment. There we hid behind the door in a corner and tested the liquor. It didn't taste like anything we had ever put to our mouth before and burned the lips and tongue like Mexican hot sauce. The cook was still cleaning up the galley so one of the men went to him and asked for some orange juice. He was a friend of the cook so he returned with the keys to our bulk storage. Several of the guys went with him to get the orange juice and when they returned with several boxes of crackers, pork and beans, and spam, I knew we were wrong and fixing to get into some trouble. There had been so many problems keeping this ship going until I had almost given up and was beginning to decide to join the rest of the crew rather than go it alone. We mixed the quart of white liquor into a half gallon of orange juice and proceeded to have us a picnic there in the dark. We started off whispering to each other and I don't remember when we started yelling but I sure couldn't forget the fact I was on report the next day. We were all scheduled for captains mast but it was delayed due to continued engine room and steering problems which had started since we left San Juan. Things kind of quieted down about the mast and we eased the big L.S.T. into the mouth of a small bay at Ciadad Trijilluo, now known as Santa Domingo in The Dominican Republic. After tying the ship to the small pier we were notified half the crew could have liberty tonight and the other half tomorrow evening. We were leaving in two days so even if I did want to go ashore there wasn't any chance. My I.D. and liberty card along with the small amount of money I had was lifted off me back in San Juan and on top of that I was restricted to the ship pending captain mast. I doubled on duty the first night, then the following afternoon my friend, who was in the same situation as me, suggested we talk to our division officer about fishing from the pier. He agreed but said, "Only the pier", so we headed out to see the cook about some bait. When we went to cold storage looking for something to fish with we found frozen shrimp packed in 5 pound boxes. Since the shrimp was frozen hard and couldn't be broken, the cook reluctantly allowed us to have a full box. We got our fishing tackle and headed for the pier but after not getting any bites in the first hour we asked a local native who was sitting in a small paddle boat if he would carry us across the river to those rocks. Surely the fishing would be better over there. We both had some change and gave him a quarter each for the trip. No one from the ship even noticed and all was going well, so I placed the box of shrimp in the waters edge to thaw out and we climbed out on a rock to try out luck. Behind us was a high cliff with paths worn in and around the rocks as they weaved to the top, but there wasn't anyone nearby. Over here it seemed the fish didn't want out bait either so I turned and asked my buddy if he would like trying a spot further down toward the shore. At that time I saw a large black man eating our shrimp. He had squatted in the waters edge very scantly dressed and was picking out the shrimp one at a time and eating them shell and all. I yelled for him to get away but he paid me no mind so I reeled in my hook and started toward him. He grabbed the box from the water and moved toward the cliff bottom. At that time several other black men came from the bushes at the base of the cliff and joined him, all of them grabbing and trying to break the frozen shrimp apart. I looked across the river and couldn't see anyone on the L.S.T. to signal or try yelling for help nor could I see the small boat which brought us over there. By this time the men had surrounded my buddy and I and had taken our fishing tackle. They ate the shrimp off the hooks which we were using for bait and some were licking the shrimp box which they had torn into several pieces. They were talking and mumbling about something, but neither my buddy nor I could understand their language. Finally one of them decided he was the leader and began making gestures and motions for us to come with them up the cliff. I told my buddy any attempt to run now might cause us both to get hurt so let's go along with them until we had a better chance of getaway. He asked, "Getaway to where?" Neither of us had any idea of which way to go except into the water. A couple of big hands on both of my arms had convinced me to climb the cliff with these nice people and I began telling them how much I appreciated their hospitality. About halfway up the cliff several of the men stopped and the rest went on. After a few minutes of jabbering they motioned for us to move on as if they had stopped to let us rest. As we reached the cliffs top I was amazed at the view ahead. The top tapered down as if into a small valley and there was a large village of make shift houses and litter. The cliff top was shaped in such a manner you couldn't see the village from the sea nor from across the river where the city lay. The men pushed us into one of the houses by the cliff edge and sat us on a wooden shipping crate. They went and brought back a weird looking round table. Then two of them pulled in another box and sat down across from my buddy and me. We began at the same time to explain to them that we had no money to give or to play cards with, if this was what they were intending. They only sat there and chattered at each other and paid us no mind. We were both ringing wet with sweat, so one of them went someplace and came back with a galvanized pail full of water, which looked like an elephant had stepped on it. When we both refused the water they poured it on our heads. Although it may have only been a few minutes it seemed like hours to me before anything different from their chatter took place. Suddenly, someone removed the door and in came two black women. Both looked to be about eight months pregnant and were twice our age. They took the place of the two men who were sitting across from my buddy and me and all the men began to leave the house. As I looked around the one room house I could see eyes peaking through all the holes in the walls. I explained to the women we were sailors and must return to our ship right away and we didn't have any money. We both stood to empty our pockets as proof and they yelled something as they pointed for us to sit down. I asked them to speak English or get someone who understood us but they wouldn't listen and kept yelling and pointing to the table. By now, the sun was going down and at a glance you could tell there was no light of any kind available and pretty soon we were going to be among these nice people in darkness. I knew we had to take a chance on their understanding what we were saying but we had to do something soon or our ship's crew may never hear from us again. I began discussing an escape plan with my buddy. All the time we were talking we looked toward the two women so as not to arouse suspicion in the men waiting outside. We decided the element of surprise was the best and probably only chance we had of escaping. I would count to three in a normal voice and on three I would lung through the door to my left and he would do the same through the door on his right. Once outside we would run for our lives and would see each other whenever. Slowly I began to count and when I said three both doors flew off that house as if they had only been propped up and I went flying over the edge of the cliff still running in mid air and I thought, oh my goodness, I've picked the wrong door as I bounced off the side of a slope which was loaded with cans, bottles, animal bones, and trash of all sorts. I scaled the side of the cliff like a skier coming off the side of Mt. Everest with a herd of polar bears chasing him. When I finally tumbled to a stop, I began running and fighting my way through vines. Then tumbling and falling, until I reached the beach. It was dusk dark and I could see the ship so I ran along the river on the opposite side. After traveling about a half mile up the river I could see a bridge which crossed over into the city. I began winding my way back up the cliff which now wasn't so steep. When I reached flat land I could see the road leading to the bridge. Once in the road I noticed I was all alone and couldn't see a human moving any place. As I ran upon the entrance to the bridge there was a long wooden arm extended across the road and when I ran around it, a guard ran out yelling. I just kept going and when I reached the other side another guard was there but he didn't pay me any attention. After arriving in town I came upon some men from my ship and they took me back in a taxi. After the drunk medic sewed up my cuts and patched my wounds the chief boatswain mate placed me on report for the second time in two weeks. Now I had two captain's mast coming and I knew my buddy was out there in trouble so I told the chief what had happened. He said, that's too bad because the shore patrol can't even go into that place, it is a village where they put all the people who want to overthrow the government. Later that night my buddy arrived safely and he was also placed on report. He said he was running through all those make shift houses trying to elude a large group of men when a man called to him in English. He ran into the man's house and the man made all the ones chasing him go away. This man was from Scotland and offered him food and water. I asked if he talked with the Scot about what those people wanted and he said the man wouldn't discuss it with him but walked him to the bridge where he told the guard to call the shore patrol and they returned him to the ship.

The following morning we left the Dominican Republic and headed out to sea then turned north. The twelve small mine sweepers encircled the L.S.T. like worker bees around their queen and sliced through the bright blue water with the greatest of ease. At a distance they looked like miniature battleships but to this huge body of water, they were no more than kids toys in the bath tub. Our main engines continued to give problems and we had decreased our maximum speed to less than 7 knots (9.8 m.p.h.) plus our port generator had begun smoking heavily. Our original schedule would put us arriving at Charleston in nine days but this was already being updated due to engine problems. In the evening of the third day at sea the barometer began dropping, clouds were rolling in from the north and the sea looked very different from before. It appeared as if angry and with the wind increasing the water was spraying around the ship's bow like a huge mustache. The crew had been ordered to secure her for heavy seas and they were lashing and chaining everything down which might shift or roll about the ship. Most every man had sensed the impending dangers ahead and for once, was realizing the many things which should have been done months ago. The ship was far from sea worthy and the storm would no doubt give her great punishment. By ten p.m. that third day out the crew had been placed in a double security network within the ship and every effort would be made to provide damage control and communications to the bridge. Around two a.m. the following morning the sea seemed to calm slightly but our barometer maintained below normal readings. The forth day remained slack and the crew continued buttoning up every loose end which they could find. Top side movement had not been restricted, although occasional over spray kept the main deck wet and slippery. I could see the mine sweepers bobbing up and down but they had widened their distance to about 500 yards apart. They looked like they had been abandoned and virtually no one could be seen on them. During the forth night, the seas gradually increased in height and continued to increase on the fifth day. Out problems with the engines and the port generator seemed to increase in proportion to the storm and on the fifth night, top side movement was forbidden outside the ship's hull. During my patrol of the ship I would report any unusual happening to the duty officer in the ship's pilot house every hour and when I arrived to make the 2300 (11 p.m.) report, the duty officer was calling the captain. Our captain was the senior officer afloat and the officer was telling him about a mine sweeper to our rear which had reported what he thought was a man yelling for help off the sweeper's starboard side. Our captain arrived in the pilot house almost immediately and called radio central. He told them to radio each sweeper and ordered an immediate muster of their crews. General quarters was sounded on the L.S.T. and everyone was accounted for on our ship but when I returned to the pilot house I heard them saying one of the sweepers up ahead had a man missing. He was a second class quartermaster and had left the sweepers pilot house to get wet bulb and barometer readings. The speaker in our pilot house was now reporting the radio message of the sweeper ahead and the man had been thrown in the ocean carrying away a section of the aluminum life rail which encircled the sweeper's weather station. Our ship had now reduced speed on orders from the captain to only enough power to hold her bow into the oncoming stormy seas and high winds. He was talking with the sweep captains about their ships ability to come about in the heavy seas and they were going to attempt turning. If successful in turning around without capsizing they would proceed at flank speed to 20 miles south then form a line and scan from east and west across one mile of water using their large search lights. They were successful in their turn and were all heading back past the L.S.T. at the maximum speed of their engines. Some of them were already manning the large spot lights on both sides of their boats. No one on our ship slept that night and as we wallered and tossed in the ocean I watched the sweepers behind us almost on the horizon as their huge lights cut through the dark sky and sea spray in a desperate attempt to save this man's life. The sea was tossing the small sweepers in such a manner that the hard to control spot lights seemed to be searching the sky or sending out weird flashing signals. You could see the anxiety of those watching the lights as they hoped any minute now, the lights will go out and we will know they have him back safely. Many thoughts ran through my mind as to what I'd be thinking if I was in that dark, angry sea. Encouraging reports kept coming back from the sweepers of the good swimmer the man was and his Mae West life jacket would hold him up for at least 12 hours and they kept reporting false sightings. As day broke on the sixth day we were still wallering in the heavy seas and the sweepers reports were getting less encouraging. I had welded a stool to the deck in damage control central before the storm, so I sat on it and rested my head on the steel table. I had almost dozed off when a call came from the bridge asking me to take some men and check the stern of the ship. The officer said our speed had been dragged down to zero and even when he put extra power to the ship it would not move, and he could only maintain a heading into the storm. When I reached the stern with two other men it had begun to rain hard and you could no longer see anything behind the ship. I watched the sea water roll over the stern in one foot deep sheets and knew something was dragging us down, I sent one of the men below to check for flooding and as I held on to the water tight door looking at the stern, I saw the large stern anchor winch rotate. At first I thought I was seeing things then I realized our huge beaching anchor wasn't locked in it's housing. As a matter of fact, it wasn't on the ship at all. I ran back to central station and notified the bridge we had lost or was loosing our beaching anchor. The captain had arrived on the bridge and he wanted to know how much cable was out. A quick check of the cable indicated it was approaching 50 fathoms,(150 feet) and the captain said he was coming down for me to stand by. He arrived with the deck officer and they readily saw what was holding the ship back. This anchor dragging through the water would require more power than our ship had to pull it. Our winch motor had burned out when we lifted the landing craft back in San Juan. So the captain said we had no choice except to cut the cable because when the anchor reached the ocean bottom it would jerk a section of the ships stern out. I put my life jacket on and sent one man for a portable cutting torch. With a line tied around my waist I crawled across the ships stern while dragging the cutting outfit behind. When I reached the winch I tried tightening the large brake wheel but couldn't get the cable to quit slipping. I lay down behind the large brake box and tied myself to its base. The ocean had a powerful force when it hit my body and I would shift quickly if not holding on or tied down to something. I lit the torch with an igniter and placed it over the 3 inch diameter cable. As each strand popped it sizzled through the air around me and unraveled out of sight in both directions along the main cable body. I continued to cut one stand at a time while reaching out the full extent of my arm and shielding my face behind the brake box. Suddenly, after I had cut about half way through, the strands began to pop, then they went in rapid succession. I backed away as far as I could but the strand were spiraling out almost 10 feet and were cutting at me from every direction. They wound up in my torch and carried it out of my hand ripping the oxygen and acetylene hose away from the bottles. When another man arrived to rescue me, the strands had wound into my hair and clothing pulling me up against the winch and pinning me down like I had been caught by an octopus. The anchor was gone but there would be a problem getting me loose form the cable. Later a man was sent out on the second man's line and began cutting me loose with a set of bolt cutters. Afterwards I was dragged across the stern and pulled inside, then carried to sick bay. Our medic was sober, for a change, and he patched me up again, grumbling as if he was getting tired of seeing me down there. Back up on deck I heard of aircraft arriving during the day to help search for the missing quartermaster but there had not been any success. They were out of Guantanimo Bay, Cuba and had returned to base due to weather conditions. By law a search must be conducted for 24 hours, so the sweepers would be returning by midnight. In the meantime we continued to waller in the heavy seas. At around 8 p.m. on the sixth day the L.S.T. went back to making some speed and the sea calmed during the night. The following day the mine sweepers rejoined us and we attempted to highline some provisions to each of them. With some of them we were successful but others had to cut away. The sea was almost calm but the rain came in torrents and at times you could hardly see the sweeper alongside. The engineers working below in the generator room had severed our port generator and lit off the starboard unit. Apparently it was in bad shape also because black smoke was now rolling out the starboard exhaust. One of the crew members who was helping with the highline operation told me the barometer was way down and according to radar we were in the eye of a hurricane. He said the storm was moving in the same direction as the ships and as long as we remained in its eye we would be safe. Late that evening I heard the engineers light off our port generator and looked over the side. There wasn't anymore black smoke from that side, so I knew for sure they had gotten it fixed but after it ran for about five minutes there was a loud bang and it stopped. An investigation revealed a gasket which was replaced in the lube oil line didn't have any hole in it and the engine had thrown a rod through the side. There seemed to be incompetence from every angle we turned and most were small items which led to major problems. Early the next morning the storm changed course and we were caught up in a ride it out or sink situation. It wouldn't be easy to swamp the flat bottom L.S.T., but the ship would go with the cross current in such erratic directions it was virtually impossible to steer a specific course. The compass was swinging from complete north to south so the only thing to do was maintain a heading into the raging sea. The mine sweepers were now on their own and would have to survive at their best individual capabilities. They had split up and headed out alone in whatever direction they could steer. The seas were leaping over our bow and ripping away the topside ventilation intakes which had rusted away from the ship's main deck. Water was pouring down through these systems and into all compartments below. Wadding in knee deep water on the tank deck we rigged emergency pumps to every outboard discharge we could find and it became a full time job keeping floating objects from clogging the pump strainers. During the day and night we lost track of time and teamed up in a futile effort to save our lives by saving our ship. From the pilot house you could see the bow drop and rise as if the ship had a spring in the center but this L.S.T. didn't have any expansion joints so this was steel bending and flexing within its own structure. How long before fatigue would cause a rupture in the hull was anyone's guess. Our small boiler had been shut down unable to function and just as well, since the evaporators weren't making any water to amount to anything anyway. All cooking had discontinued and sandwiches were distributed along with coffee to the crew. Most all the equipment which had been lashed down was breaking loose and either floating, rolling or tumbling about the ship on all levels. I'm not sure how many days and nights we fought this storm but it began to slowly subside in the same manner it had started and the crew began grabbing a few winks of sleep every place they could find a dry spot. When topside restrictions of movement were finally lifted and we began going out on deck with lines hooked to our waist in an effort to assess topside damage, I was surprised and relieved to see a 2250 class destroyer standing off to our port side. After making my way around the superstructure I waved at another destroyer which was standing off to our starboard side. These beautiful storm riders I learned had been with us for the last four days. There was no sign of the mine sweepers and I heard they were safe and would meet us in Charleston. There were many tales to be told about that terrible storm but I thought one of the most fascinating was when the navigator told us of hour after hour when he was actually reporting the ship's position as much as a mile back from its position the hour before. During that day we barely made any time and everyone worked hard scuttling away broken vents and ruined equipment into piles on the tank deck. We had come away from the hurricane which would lash the North Carolina coast within a few hours, with no more than one main engine, a starboard generator smoking heavily, and our lives, but I believe there was much more in the great lesson everyone had learned. The destroyers left us that evening and early the next day a large sea going tug came into view on the horizon. By nightfall we had been taken in tow by the tug and the following day we anchored in the mouth of Ashley River. For the first time I found out what day it was and we had left the Dominican Republic 18 days ago. Later that day we were allowed to enter the harbor under our own power and tied the ship to a pier at the old minecraft base. The mine sweepers were there and they didn't look like the sleek little battleships I had seen in the Caribbean Sea. They were all severely damaged topside, and some had been completely striped of their mast and radar equipment. Within the next few days everyone aboard the L.S.T. received transfer orders to all points of the globe and it had been determined that this ship had made her last trip on the open seas. She was being tagged for towing and would be cut into scrap. I met several of these men in different countries over the next years and from what I could learn of their reputation it had improved greatly as a result of our almost fatal cruise in the Caribbean Sea. I never saw my friend again, who like myself had two captain mast coming and I never heard of the mast again.

"THUNDER IN IRAN"

After spending almost 21 years in the U.S. Navy, with 17 of these years at sea, I should not feel any different while waiting at Dallas International Airport in Washington, D.C. to board the huge gray Pan Am 747 SP for Tehran, Iran, but there was a difference. Although I had visited most every country in the eastern hemisphere there was a different feeling about this journey into Iran. There is no way to describe my immediate attitude except I had a lesser feeling of authority, respect and prestige which hovered over me like a dark cloud.

The next thirty-three hours put me nine hours ahead of all those friends whom I had left behind. My year of arrival was 2332 causing me to be 399 years old and for the next two weeks my eating and sleeping patterns seemed to be reversed. Friday was now to be Sunday, the month had another name and instead of arriving on the 24th of February, I had arrived on the 11 of Jamada-1. Calendars are not available, so you can imagine how confused one from the west would be in about two weeks.

Tehran was the scene of many high rise concrete and steel structures at various construction stages and there was a snow capped mountain peak visible to the north. There was green grass and some sort of thorny trees growing throughout the city and for the most part, there was a fairly good attitude among the Iranians toward foreigners. After walking about town you could readily see why people didn't recommend riding in taxis, by the amount of strewn vehicles which had been involved in head on collisions. It looked as if taxis made up about 60% of these collisions. There was a Kentucky Fried Chicken on one corner and a Burger King on the other, so for the first day I seemed pretty much at ease. After security clearance and all the documents of my identification had been processed, I was taken to Tehran Domestic Airport and put aboard and Iran air DC-8 bound for Bandar Abbas. Bandar, meaning sea port and then the town of Abbas was located 960 miles south of Tehran on the Persian Gulf. The passengers on the DC-8 carried a variety of carry on luggage and the law of placing it under the seat in front of you wasn't the case this time. The man alongside me had five chickens with their legs tied together and up front there were several sheep. It wasn't all that bad once we were air born because from the announcements, I had gathered the pilot and one stewardess were American.

Bandar Abbas lies just south of a high mountain range and directly along the sea. This meant no cool winds from the north blew there and when the night breeze came from the sea it must rise up and over the town, thus there was a lull of hot humid stillness lurking here forever. This had been the location of the most dreaded prison existing in Iran and for over three hundred years men had been given a choice, either go to prison at Bandar Abbas or be beheaded. Most had chosen to be beheaded and I was about to find out why. As the plane began to descend I could see a mass of grayish brown below. There wasn't a cloud in the sky and from the looks of this mass at an even height, extending as far as you could see across the horizon, I knew it wasn't moisture, yet it appeared to be a muddy lake with steam rising from its surface. When the plane entered this shield of sorts, there was a shaking motion and some darkness but within seconds it emerged into another clear area and you could now plainly see the mountain peaks below. Looking up, I noticed the sun being dimmer, but was shinning through the mass. Below lie huge jagged spikes of mountain tops, brown and baron, no signs of life of any sort, and these peaks looked as if they had been shaped by the receding sea. Just as the stewardess announced, "No further smoking until after entry into the terminal." The plane shot from between the mountain peaks and I could see a flat, brown deserted landscape below. A few minutes later I stepped out of the DC-8 into a still 118 degree fahrenhiet temperature and 100% humidity. My brain didn't have to direct my body to cover itself with water and I was soaked within minutes. I knew now why many men from the west had arrived to work at Bandar Abbas and had left on the same plane that flew them in but I was bound and determined to stick it out since I had come this far. It already seemed as if I had left home a month ago and I dreaded making that 8,000 mile trip again in the near future. Customs and immigration were no problem as long as you kept your mouth shut. No one understood the others language anyway and they didn't care who came there but leaving there would be the problem.

When I arrived at my companies leased quarters there was one Iranian guard on the only gate in or out and the building looked like one brown concrete block with a bunch of doors and a small air conditioner sticking in a hole through the wall. Once inside, I realized that's what it was and if you didn't have electric power you had better have some other source of light or you were in total darkness. The screen and large wooden doors had been fitted with leather sealer pads at the bottoms of each. I thought these were for keeping out dust but couldn't figure why they didn't extend all the way around, however, at my first briefing I was told of another reason. The sealer pads were to keep out the deadly poisonous and painful black scorpion. The yellow one wasn't to be feared but if hit by the larger black one, you must treat the wound as a rattler bite. In all cases you must be hospitalized. I was told to shake my shoes out in the mornings before placing my feet into them because the scorpion would enter seeking coolness but when he became cold he would crawl into the dark shoes. Power failures were frequent and I was advised to purchase a battery lantern which was available on the local market. I didn't get any answer to my question about air conditioning when a power failure occurred. The camp administrator complained about someone stealing the only chair in my room and said he owed me a pillow cover and a sheet, of which I never received. There was a small shelf in the rest room and this could be used to hold the portable gas stove for cooking my food. A hole had been made in there with a sledge hammer for venting the rest room and this offered the only vent for cooking available. I could purchase a T.V. or radio locally, but could only see or hear Persian because Dubia and Abu Daubi located in the United Arab imarants across the Gulf were too far to reach. Also, it was recommended that I buy a refrigerator because ice was extremely hard to find. If ice was found it would probably make me sick and I wasn't to drink water outside the camp or the ship yard while at work. Pepsi could be purchased by the bottle, but most of these had gum, cigarette butts or roaches in the bottom and some were only half full or less of drink. The company had set up a small meeting hall for the men who had been authorized by the Shaw's government, however most of the time there was no cooling facilities for the beer. A local black market booze was an 18% alcoholic Vodka and I mean alcoholic because that's what happened to everyone who drank this stuff. All foods were bought locally but fresh meat was only available in the form of chicken or maybe occasionally fish, if a boat came in. There were plenty of fresh vegetables in town but they had to be soaked for two hours in a special chemical, then thoroughly washed before eating. The runs was a common occurrence and medication for this was standard issue. Total company recreation centered around one swimming pool and a purification pump had failed in that with no spare parts available. The picture kind of looked like the captain had bailed out and left the crew with a sinking ship, but to me, it was a new challenge and I was eager to move ahead.

Transportation to and from work at the Imperial Iranian Navel Shipyard was in six minibuses driven by ex-Kami Kazi pilots. During these trips it wasn't unusual to see a car pass then pull in and knock a bike rider 50 yards into the desert. The Iranians used dump trucks which they called lorries to haul wheat from the sea port inland and they didn't bother to block off the large holes around the dump door. He may leave the ship with 18 tons and arrive to load off 100 miles away with only a couple of hundred pounds of wheat left, however the next trip would be a repeat performance. Iranian women clad in black from head to foot would come out at night to sweep the wheat from the edge of the road. They needed wheat for bread and to feed their goats so they would scoot along on their rear and gather the wheat into small piles with tiny brooms made of grass. Later they would collect the small piles into sacks but for some it was much, much later. Early each morning enroute to work I would look for them alongside the road or in the desert and hardly a week would pass before I would see one and sometimes two lying along the road. Vehicles traveling at night would hit them and they were very dead. Many times I have seen one in the morning and she would still be lying there when we returned from work late that evening. At one point, on this road leading to the sea port, was a narrow bridge over a small gorge, which extended from the mountains to the gulf. At low tide it looked like a dried up creek bed but at high tide it would be waist deep with sea water. One morning two lorries collided on the narrow bridge. It took about one hour to get the trucks separated and moving again, but it took the police through the day and night to clear the traffic jam caused by Iranians spearpointing the narrow crossing. Apparently these people feel if they have to drive someplace there should be no obstruction in their path. When an Iranian vehicle stalls on the road by any cause, he will roll large boulders and place them around it to protect it from fast oncoming traffic, however when he makes repairs and leaves, he does not remove the boulders and during one night as many as twenty five people will die as a result of colliding with the stones.

Speaking of rock piles there was another one of sorts that I knew of in Iran. It was located about 30 miles north of Bandar Abbas at the foot of the mountains and was enclosed by a high security fence woven of barbed wire. Rock pile was probably a trade name or cover but it was allowed under the Shaw's regime and was guarded by the Gestapo or Shaw's secret police. There were two gates which you must pass through to enter, one at the security fence and another at the high private fence which enclosed the little town from any public view. You identified at the first gate and paid at the second. Inside there was all the gaiety of another world, gambling, whiskey, girls, sports, hash hish, cocaine or whatever you desired was made available for a price. Everything was brought in by the Shaw's police force and the girls were slaves of trade from Afghanistan, Pakistan, India, Egypt, U.A.E., and some solid whites from Yugoslavia and Russia. Of course when Komeni arrived and declared marshall law this was one of the first places surrounded by his national army troops but by then the Iranians had fell in love with all the girls and ran the foreigners out, so it was young slave girls and Iranian nationals who lost their heads in the 700 person human slaughter that day.

Meanwhile, back on the home front, I had found a small

brown male puppy in the ship yard during my second week there and had smuggled him out the gate inside my shirt. He didn't like my cooked chicken to well and neither did I, so I started buying some of the steak shipped in from Australia which only a dog could eat anyway. He liked that and began to grow so I kept him inside most of the time out of sight of any Iranians. They considered the dog as a disease and my problems started when I noticed it had been over a week and my room wasn't swept. Sand is tracked in daily and after a while it began to pile up. I could sweep it myself and didn't mind if I had the equipment. I spoke to the camp manager and he told me the old Iranian women of hire to clean the rooms won't come into a place with a dog there. Sam was every bit of two months old and you can imagine how vicious he was. Anyway, that didn't matter because Sam and I would do our own cleaning and washing. I left him locked in my room and would go into town after dark or before daylight and shop for food. If you tried to walk there during the day you might have a heat stroke and several times at night I almost had a stroke while diving from the side walk to avoid being hit by a motor bike or Toyota truck. I believe if you tied a thread on back of an Iranian Toyota truck and stuck a needle up the side walk he could thread that needle. When I bought chickens I always bought them on the hoof. You pick out the one you want and point it out to the kid wading around barefoot among them. He would ring its neck and throw it outside along with the head. When you handed it to the shop owner he would point for you to give him the head also. He put these in a large set of baby scales and began balancing with rocks, spark plugs, horse shoes, nails and what have you, until the scales were even. For the life of me I never figured out how he determined the price. I know I paid 10 to 1 in ratio to the Iranian but if an Iranian got caught shopping for an American, off came his head, so I understood that much about the price. What really got confusing was when you bought a large watermelon, because sometimes he would have you wait while he went into the desert and gathered rocks to use for weighing it. Normally, I would pluck the feathers from the chicken while traveling back to my room and with the humidity you still got feathers stuck all over your face and hands but if I waited and plucked it in my room, well this was another mess. I once saw a cooked young hen which was packed in a can at Rochester, N.Y. I bought it from the Iranian shop keeper and when I figured my riyals, I have paid him $37.00 for two pounds of chicken and broth. I made this one last me for a week and I have to admit it was good. I had bought a small refrigerator from a man who had a Chinese wife. They were leaving Iran for good so they sold out everything. I also bought his radio and t.v. so I could get a package deal of $1900.00 for the three items, about

$1300.00 over western prices for the same thing. When I went to put washed vegetables into the bottom of the refrigerator, I noticed the couple had forgotten to remove a one half gallon jug of something. When I removed the lid it instantly paralyzed my nostrils, put out both my running lights and took my breath. I know its human nature to stick your nose into everything, but I won't do it again. I managed to get the lid back on before this thing completely consumed my room then I took it to the manager. Something with a flavor such as this could very well be some sort of bomb but he said the Chinese woman brewed a sauce called nookmom which consists of small raw fish and leaves mixed together and let set in the sun until the mixture rotted forming a liquid. Needless to say I left it with him for disposal.

I was completing my first month's work at the ship yard and didn't foresee any major problems other than dreading the heat and humidity. When I returned to my room one evening and found the power had been off all day. I didn't dare open my refrigerator so as to preserve the temperature inside and save my meat. Sam and I had soup and crackers that night and I sat outside watching him romp in the 108 degree temperature until about midnight. Still no power, so I left the battery light on and closed the screen door. At around two in the morning the world dropped about two inches. That was the sharpest sound of thunder I had ever heard but it was coming from the ground instead of the sky. I was still bouncing on the springs of my bed when my brain said, get out of here fast. Sam had beat me to the screen and most everyone else was outside. Then I knew what it was that Sam was always howling about. He was very young but he knew all about earthquakes. In the next 10 months I ran out of that room 27 times and each one I was awakened and pre-warned by Sam. During one of the quakes the thunder from the ground was very low and deep but it collapsed a concrete block wall around our camp and split the Cameron Hotel in half, which was located on the waters edge about 5 minutes walking time from the camp. Several other times during the day my table and chair at the office tried to walk out before I could get out of there. I knew these things were beyond any control of mankind and talked with a man from Poland named Ted about them. He said it was probably earthquake season in Iran.

Knowing Ted, I figured he probably believed that, although he was my friend I sometimes questioned his reasoning. Most every man in this camp was running from the law for one reason or the other but Ted didn't seem like the person who would intentionally do something wrong. He was born in Poland and his parents brought him to the U.S. at age 7, so he thought well of his home country and let you know it. He had something against Yugoslavia and everything that went wrong in the world he blamed on them. I observed him one day attempting to staple his I.D. card in its plastic holder and after several tries he blamed his failure to Yugoslavia. I told him those copper coated staples didn't have strength enough to penetrate the plastic and he should use the steel ones. He left and returned with a steel packet but began rolling the stapler gun around as if confused. I noticed a small recessed button in one side of the gun and started to tell him to push there and the staple tray would shoot out for loading but knew he would tell me to buzz off to Yugoslavia if I offered any help. After a few minutes I noticed he had separated the gun, somehow into two pieces. Then suddenly he pushed the wrong thing and blam, a staple shot clear to the hilt into the bottom of his big thick thumb. I ran into the western toilet and grabbed a handful of paper from the roll. I returned just as he was taking aim with his fingers to jerk that thing out and the things he was saying about Yugoslavia cannot be written in this story. When he yanked the staple out the blood flew and I quickly wrapped his thumb in the toilet paper. I needed a good laugh but couldn't do it in front of Ted, so I went outside and walked in the dust. I laughed and cried until I had gotten two months of Iran out of my system. Shortly afterwards Ted gave us all another thrill in camp and got himself into trouble with several of the men. Ted was a pleasant person and never meant any harm but sometimes he would get into places where he shouldn't be. He was walking to his room when he noticed several men mingling around one of the rooms. He sauntered over and struck up a conversation with a man who was standing just outside the cabin door. Ted knew this man and no one told him this was a line up or ask him to go to the rear. A few minutes later another man came out of the cabin and Ted's friend told him he could go in next. Ted became confused, so his friend told him to get out 100 riyals ($67.00) and hurry up because the others were waiting. Ted didn't have 100 riyals but entered to see what it was all about and when he saw a young naked Russian girl inside he shot out the door like a bullet. Ted went directly to the camp managers room and informed him about the nasty thing these men were doing to that young girl. The manager went to the room, ran the men away, made the girl get dressed and escorted her out of camp. She cursed him out in Russian but no one knew what she was saying. The men involved got very mad at Ted and called him a dumb pollock. Later I heard the girl was a 19 year old white Russian with a pimp located in the Cameron Hotel. Her pimp had already completed her coverage of the large camps belonging to Lockheed, Brown and Root and Bell Helicopter, where she had earned enough money to buy a Boeing 747 jet plane. Her coverage of the smaller camps like ours, was a part time job and not really needed in the first place.

Sam had gotten big enough to travel with me so I decided to explore the beach with him. I hadn't been there before but could see it from the main road each time I walked into town. As we left the camp gate Sam trotted along close to me, almost as if he sensed an outside danger. When we reached the main road, I made him sit behind a bush while I checked both ways for traffic, then I broke and ran, calling back, "Hurry, Sam!" He shot across the road like a bullet. Once in the desert on the other side of the road I slowed my pace and searched along the ground for anything strange or unusual. Sam stayed close by my side with his tongue hanging out of his mouth. His short legs were traveling ten to my one and the temperature was 118 degree's farenhite. I always wore cotton clothing because any other material would be like a metal shield around your body in this heat. You had to remember the suns rays were very short and fine in the desert and your body was the only thing out there absorbing the heat. When I approached the high tide line, I thought, Oh God, what a mess. The beach was completely consumed with animal bones, tires, foam rubber, shipping crates and crude oil. A walk on the beach was like strolling through a turkey pen and I readily found the sand not to be that at all. It was fine, gluey, gray mud, which accumulated an inch thick in the bottom of my tennis shoe. Looking closely along the water's edge I found a small bone structure which looked exactly like a large snake head. I gathered some of these and later made some necklaces by drilling through the eyes and threading it on bright colored nylon cord. I gave some of these to a man returning to the U.S. and I heard he was caught with them by customs and they confiscated them. After that happened, I took one of the snake heads to an Iranian officer and he told me they were the back bone of a fish found in the Persian Gulf. I didn't wade in the water that day, but Sam did and he seemed to enjoy himself. As we walked west along the beach I noticed a long pier reaching out into the Gulf from the Cameron Hotel. Getting closer I observed the pier had two sections of security. The first two hundred feet out had a few lights overhead and was used by hotel guests, then a locked gate with woven barbed wire all around it stopped any entry to an extremely long section extending about one thousand feet into the Gulf. At the far end there was what looked like large wooden bins located just under the pier's edge. A few days later I found out these bins were used by the boats to smuggle in hash hish, cocaine and any other items desired for distribution by the Cameron Hotel's owner. I naturally never did mention this in Iran because I didn't want to die there but the way I found out wasn't very well hidden. The following Friday morning I put Sam in his pen outside and went to the Cameron Hotel. There I met with the German manager and asked for permission to fish from the hotel pier. He had some welding to be done and I could get this done at the ship yard so we swapped favors and he gave me written permission to fish from the first one hundred feet of the pier. The following night I returned after work with a cast net and hand line. I was almost challenged upon entry to the pier by a guard who was roving about the hotel grounds. He read the note and left without speaking and after catching a few minnows with the net I caught enough large fish to feed several people. I took them back to camp and the men helped me clean them and I shared with them. I didn't eat any supper that night and about two a.m. I became deathly sick. I was so sick at my stomach I couldn't stay still so I wandered outside into the heat, I couldn't seem to find comfort any place and couldn't breath properly. Our company didn't have a doctor and I figured I was going to die. The next morning I made it to the shipyard and went to the Iranian clinic. The doctor had my stomach pumped out and by now I had large lumps under both my arms and on my neck. The clinic staff gave me two shots in one arm and one in the other and a half dozen bottles of capsules and liquids to take every four hours. The doctor said I had swallowed human waste and began to ask questions. The tide had been high the night before when I was throwing that cast net and the only thing I had put in my mouth since the day before was one of the leads on the net each time I threw it. To properly throw the cast net you must hold one of the lead weights in your mouth while casting in order to get the net to spread into a circle. The doctor told me the Cameron Hotel dumped their raw human waste through a pipe line alongside their pier into the Gulf and the minnows I had caught were probably feeding around that pipe. He said if I went there at low tide the stench would be unbearable near the edge of the pier. I got well and went back the following Friday night. The temperature and humidity were almost beyond bearing that night and there was no one else out moving about. There wasn't even any traffic on the main road when I crossed. When I arrived on the pier I went to the far end near the gate to watch for some minnows there. I planned to avoid the area where I caught the minnows on my first trip. There was about three of the fifteen pier lights burning so I crouched under one of them. I sat on my minnow bucket and watched a small boat approach the end of the pier with no lights or identification. Two men began off loading plastic bags into the bins and within five minutes the boat disappeared again into the darkness of the Gulf. A few minutes later I saw two men coming onto the pier from the hotel. When they arrived at the gate one of them began unlocking the large chain while the other stood looking at me. I didn't recognize their nationality but knew they didn't look like Iranians so I stood up. I started to leave but the man motioned for me to stay put. The other man returned shortly with two plastic bags and said something to the one who had been watching me. They locked the big chain, then the man who had stood there with me handed me a sheep skin pouch and they left. I watched them enter the rear of the hotel before I looked at the pouch. I removed the band which had a seal attached around the bundle and when I looked inside I knew I was in real trouble. Those guys had paid the wrong man for a pick up so the other man must be around close by. The money in this pouch wasn't in Iranian riyals, I don't know what kind it was, but I did know I was holding a large amount of currency that didn't belong to me. At about the same time as I made my decision to get out of there fast I saw a figure of a human moving down the pier toward me from the hotel. I couldn't believe my eyes, it was a girl wearing a mini skirt. I wouldn't accept this view in Iran and in my three months there I hadn't seen a woman's face much less her arms or legs. There was no one else in site. She appeared to be out for a stroll along the pier and from that distance didn't seem to see me yet. I hovered against the gate out of the light and thought of jumping into the water and make my way to the beach but again I kept quiet, she may not see me and go away. Things didn't happen my way and as she came closer my knees began to shake. My shoes were already full of water and my clothes were soaked with perspiration. For goodness sakes, why did it have to be so hot and humid and why me. I only came here to try to catch a fish for food. The girl walked up to me as if she knew I was there all along. She squatted under the light and lifted strands of the nylon cast net, her knees pointing at me and I was looking at her bright silk panties. My knees were knocking so bad I couldn't stand and I felt faint so I stepped toward her and sat on my minnow bucket. I eased the buckets edge up from behind and slid the sheep skin pouch under it. The girl looked at me and spoke but I didn't recognize the language. She pointed at the water and lifted the net. I explained I used it for fishing but that didn't seem to interest or make any sense to her. She stood up holding the cast net and walked toward me dragging the leads across the pier. She began talking very rapidly and loud as if she was asking me questions. I motioned with my hands that I didn't understand and suddenly she swung the leader end of the cast net at my face. I ducked and jumped off the unrailed pier. When my feet hit bottom I realized the water wasn't over my head so I ran through it at an angle until I reached the muddy beach. I headed back into the desert toward the main road and without looking back I slowed to walk through the camp gate about ten minutes later. I never told anyone in

Iran about this for fear of my life and I've not heard language that sounds like the one the girl spoke that night.

June had arrived and the labor crews from Afghanistan and Pakistan had left the Bandar Abbas area for the hot summer months. They would return in October when the climate began to change. They had even carried the flies with them or if not, the fly had left the heat to the Iranians, British and Americans. The temperature was now a steady daily 138 degrees farenhite with 100 percent humidity, dropping to a cool 118 degrees at night. Even Sam couldn't stand the outside climate and stayed inside when allowed. I had forgotten about the black scorpion until one morning in early June I slid my right shoe on and instantly tried to knock a hole in the roof of my room. When the shoe hit the floor a large wood roach ran out of it. This caused me to renew my morning shoe shaking sessions and I wasn't likely to forget again.

Around the middle of June the ground began thundering and Sam began howling. For three days this continued and it seemed very deep with occurrences almost each hour. By the fourth day the rumbling had stopped and word was creeping in about an entire city of Taba, located 600 miles to our northeast had disappeared. Taba had no concrete structures and was made mostly of mud and stone buildings and many of its residences lived in houses made of date palm limbs and when a figure was released of over 37,000 people loosing their lives due to the earthquake, it was hard for me to believe, but when I saw photographs of the area, I knew how it had happened. The earth had opened up like river beds, consumed all structures and humans, then vibrated shut, leveling off above them. When the rescue teams and equipment reached Taba, the people had been buried for more than three days. Bull dozers were used to cut a three mile long, 200 feet wide and 30 foot deep gorge just outside where the city had once stood. They then pushed the city into the gorge and buried it as a mass burial of over 37,000 men, women and children. The Shaw of Iran flew to Taba by helicopter and vowed to build a new city there, but Taba would have to have new residence also, since none of the originals were left alive. This never came to be since the Shaw's reign ended less than two months later and Taba is still a flat spot in the desert.

Ramadan was approaching in all Islamic countries and most activities were being curtailed or confined within our camp. This is a thirty day fast period observed each year by Muslims and occurs when a lone star appears cradled in the first quarter of the moon. The exact time is not known, but usually in June of each year, and all eating, drinking and smoking must be stopped between 6 a.m. and 6 p.m. daily. Precautions must be taken by foreigners not to violate the Islamic law in the presence of Muslims, although they may not be bound to the custom in the privacy of their own residence. To some Iranians, their religion can be used as law to foreigners, but if they hide from the public their violations aren't detected either, so it wouldn't be uncommon to flush the toilet in the western rest room and hear the water continue to run in the fill tank. If you remove the tank cover you will find the Iranians drinking cup had floated down and blocked the plunger in the drain pipe.

A few days prior to the beginning of Ramadan many of the employees stock up on the Vodka with 18 percent alcohol and this spelled trouble within the camp. I had heard of several incidents among this rough group of men but hadn't anticipated any involvement since I intended to stay out of site. However, on Friday morning (our Sunday off), during the first week of Ramadan, I was returning from the post office to my room and I observed a man standing in the doorway of his cabin looking toward me. He was holding a bottle of Vodka and appeared drunk. His wife had arrived in Iran for a 90 day visit with him about one week ago and as I crossed the hot dust field I saw her point at me and say something to him. Whatever she said made him real mad and he jumped off the concrete platform and met me as I started around the swimming pool fence. He told me to hold up, that he wanted to talk with me. I stopped and he said, "My wife thinks you're the best thing going around here." Immediately I realized this not to be the start of a pleasant conversation, so without saying a word I turned and started to my room. Suddenly my head and face went numb as I heard a thud and I was on the ground. I jumped to my feet as the man ran into his cabin. His wife yelled, "Run ! He's gone to get a knife!" I ran to my room and got my butcher knife and returned to the spot where he had sucker punched me in the nose. The man and his wife had locked themselves into their room, so I stuck the butcher knife up in the ground alongside the pool fence and headed toward the gate. I didn't have any feeling in my face and didn't know the blood had ran down my chin and consumed most of the front of my shirt. The temperature was around 135 degrees and I was soaked with water, so any other liquid wouldn't make any difference at this time. There wasn't anyone in site except the Iranian gate guard and he ran out trying to ask me what happened. I went past him and headed into town. When I arrived at the main road, an Iranian naval officer saw me and stopped his car. I told him what happened and he carried me to the Bandar Abbas Police Station. He told the police what had happened in Persian language and they made a phone call. The naval officer asked me to come with him to a small wash room outside. He got some rags and assisted me in removing the blood from my face and neck, then we returned to the police building and he told me to wait for a few minutes. Shortly afterwards two Iranian soldiers arrived carrying side arms and automatic rifles. The police motioned for me to go with them and the naval officer followed us in a U.S. made Jeep into camp. The soldiers didn't stop at the gate, although about 15 employees and our manager were waiting for my return. They went directly through the desert to the room number which I had given them. They quickly went to the door and knocked once loudly. They kicked the door down and it fell into the room. The camp manager ran up along side with a group of other men yelling at me to tell them what happened. They said they would take care of this man for me and he would never make anymore trouble for anyone. The manager said I could stop the Iranians from taking him, but he didn't blame me, although if he went to jail it would be an international incident and the Embassy in Tehran would be notified. The naval officer took me by the hand and led me to his car. He said not to listen to the Americans because the police would take care of this man. The two soldiers dragged the man from his room while the others stood watching and he was trying to give them a handful of riyals, begging them not to take him to jail. The soldiers had put chains on his arms and legs and they literally threw him into the jeep and sped away toward town. I returned to the police station with the naval officer and he read me a document written in Persian. It told me the man's name, his past record of violence in the U.S. and he was from Gulfport Mississippi. The statement said the man was restrained by me and I was the only one who could order his release. It said he may receive food and drink from his company and friend, but would not be allowed anything under Islamic law. I was told to sign the document then I asked to see him. A policeman took me to an enclosed area and pointed to one of the many holes in the ground. The man had been forced to climb down a ladder into a six foot square hole, twenty foot deep and he sat on the ground. He didn't look up, so I returned to the police room and the naval officer brought me back to the camp. The manager said the man's wife was packing their personal belongings and she wanted to talk with me, but I refused. The manager also said if I would sign a release this man would be flown out of Bandar Abbas the following morning, so I signed the release and never saw the man or his wife again. When I arrived at the ship yard the next morning I was sent to the ship yard clinic. Head x-rays showed my nose broken in three separate locations from the top to the base. The doctor packed it and said that was all they could do for this type of injury and I could hope it would heal back straight. That evening I found my butcher knife by the swimming pool fence but I never found the letter I was carrying when the man hit me. It was a letter from my mom and the only thing I ever knew of it was the postmark date, which told me it had taken 27 days to reach me in Iran.

At the same time when all this mess was taking place I was notified of an emergency call from the United States. When I came to the camp at noon the manager said the party left no message. Then when I returned to the shipyard, I was called to the commander's office and told an emergency call had come in through the Persian phone system at the yard from the U.S. He told me to return to camp and place a call to the states though the company charge system, which would be billed to my wages. I returned to camp and gave the Iranian radio operator the number of a good friend and Southern Bell Telephone operator whom I knew in Georgia. I was afraid to call my mother because I felt something had happened to her. The Iranian said he would put me through in 30 minutes, but as every 45 minutes passed that afternoon, he told me it would be another 30 more minutes. I hadn't eaten any breakfast or lunch that day and was extremely upset, so I ordered the company secretary to get me a flight out of Iran. She was trying to secure passage out through Dubai, then to Saudi Arabia, where I could get a direct flight to the U.S. If I must go out through Tehran I would have a one day lay over and could not get to the states in an emergency. At about 3 p.m. the Iranian said my call was coming from the U.S., but when I answered the operator was asking for another man. I told her he wasn't there and asked her to place an emergency call to the operator in Georgia and ask the operator to call me in Iran. She said that was against the law and disconnected me. A few minutes later the man arrived and said to me an emergency call came in at the ship yard for me at about 2 p.m. He said he had talked to the operator and they were placing the call again at 5 p.m. to me at this number, so for me to stand by there. As it would have to happen, the Iranian operator yells to me that the call in the United States is now ringing. I picked up the phone as someone said hello. It didn't take a minute to realize the number I had given the Iranian operator had too many sevens in it for him to comprehend and he had gotten me into the right state but wrong city. I was connected with a black woman's residence in Macon, Georgia about seventy miles from the intended party. This woman is uptight about prank callers and she had labeled me as one of those. She has never heard of a place called Iran and she wants to know weather I'm a black boy or a white boy. After begging for five minutes she agreed to go next door and ask her neighbor's advice about her calling someone for me. She returned and told me her neighbor wasn't home and she wasn't sure about what to do, so I hung the phone up. That call cost me $56.00 and the woman in Macon never placed a call for me. I was worried sick and becoming dizzy by 5 p.m. when sharply the call came. It was my good friend who worked with Southern Bell in Athens, Georgia and she told me my parental uncle had died suddenly of a heart attack. I sighed with tremendous relief, to know my mother was o.k. although I loved my uncle very much. Even in the time it had taken to reach me with the message, much less the trip to the U.S. if I had gone, would have no bearing on the past funeral services.

With Ramandan in full swing the company recreation committee had finally found enough funds to allow the men to take a trip to an oasis at the edge of the mountains and I was one of the first to sign up. The manager said $40.00 was deducted from each employee's pay after each month for their recreation fund but someone had been stealing this money. I enjoyed the trip since it was my first outside of Bandar Abbas since arrival in February. I got a chance to see the place they called the rock pile and saw some camels along the way. The sun was very hot that day but the scene of the oasis, its people and sharing cold Pepsi's and sandwiches made a good outing. At the beginning of the oasis, was the sacred pool where the women bathed their bodies and the men bathed in any other place of depth along the stream. The water temperature was 170 degrees when it sprang from the ground and I could imagine there must be a large fire burning some place under this brown dust. There were large water traps, crudely devised thousands of years ago which gave evidence of humans trying to capture the precious liquid. I was approached by a young Iranian girl, seeking the handout of a cold Pepsi and she wasn't wearing the traditional Muslim head gear. I couldn't believe the beauty in her face and the perfect shape of her body. The thought ran through my mind of her suddenly throwing away her shabby clothing and becoming one of the most beautiful stars in Hollywood. I guessed that would be a first for the Islamic countries. While at the oasis I observed a shepherd eating bread under a tree while his sheep grazed and drank at the stream. After he left, another came and removed the bread from the tree, ate some, then placed it back into the tree limbs. I later discussed this with a naval officer and questioned their eating during Ramadan. According to him Ramadan is a time of obedience to Allah and is based upon individual religious beliefs. As for sharing the bread it is Gods will among hungry neighbors and those who share will never perish.

During the remainder of Ramadan I stayed in my room weaving nets for crab traps and when it ended, I took some chicken necks to the sea wall at Bandar Abbas. My first trip netted several large Blue Claw crabs, which were very delicious. When I went back, I began gathering a crowd and within two weeks the sea wall was loaded with Iranians gathering crabs for food, day and night. I made many friends among those people and they wouldn't steal from me, but they believed in borrowing, so most of the time I didn't have a net left to catch crabs for myself. Finally, they began showing up with their own, which they had copied from my design. An Iranian will do anything for food to feed his family, but he won't do remedial work for money, so they catch on to hunting and fishing techniques very fast.

My company received an invitation from one of the provincial chiefs in the mountains to go on a wild boar hunt and I signed up to go along, but when I found out I was a stick carrier instead of a gun carrier, I quickly scratched the trip. Several men went and no one got hurt, also they got one large hog, which the chief let them keep and we had a nice cook out. But I'll never know what might have happened that day if I had gone along on the hunt. Wild boars in Iran will destroy a man in a few seconds just for thrill much the less if you herd him into a trap with a stick.

In July our international superintendent at Tehran sent his wife to Bandar Abbas for an audit of company policy and she told me to go to Tehran and apply for food at the Embassy Commissary. My military retired status made me eligible for this privilege, which would cut my food cost in half. I would mail an air force wife the food list each month and send her two signed checks on a U.S. bank. One was for the food, the other was for shopping fee, transportation and bus service to deliver the food to Bandar Abbas. I wanted to get this privilege, if for nothing else, they sold Camel cigarettes in the commissary and these weren't available any other place in Iran. I had been tearing the filter off Winstons since two weeks after my arrival over there. I purchased a ticket with Iran air to Tehran and return but wouldn't you know, it was the same flight the lady was returning on. She had gone out to the desert around Bandar Abbas and gathered a large bag of rocks. The rocks didn't look unusual to me but she said she wanted to study their structure. Of course, the bag was too heavy for her to carry so I ended up going through customs with them. In Bandar Abbas the customs officials search your body for all flights, so women enter through one enclosure and the men through another. When I entered about the only thing this dude was interested in, was that bag of rocks. He let me know, in no uncertain terms, that I couldn't go wandering off with a bag of rocks in Bandar Abbas like I owned the joint. I got frustrated with him and gave him the rocks by pouring them all out on his table, then I tromped out the exit with the bag in hand. Just outside the door a guard stuck his handgun up my nose and marched me right back inside the room. He motioned for me to put those rocks back into the bag and after I did that he motioned for me to get out. On the plane

I sat with that old lady and I told her she would have to carry her rocks through customs in Tehran. I didn't mind carrying all her luggage but I had had it with those goofy rocks. We got through o.k. at Tehran and they acted as if they wouldn't have cared if you came dragging the plane through with you. I got my shopping permit and talked with the superintendent before returning to Bandar Abbas. He was worried about something coming down in Iran and had rumors of the Shaw's disappearance. He said he had lost contact with the Iranian Atomic Energy Commission, of which was responsible for my monthly radiation dosage printouts. I was handling two radioactive isotopes for training Iranians at the navy ship yard and these materials were becoming an alarming issue among the old Islamic population. I told him I'd keep my eyes and ears open, then I returned to Bandar Abbas. The following week I was called by the Imperial Iranian Navy Ship Yard Commander. He told me of the disappearance of the Shaw and of some high ranking officials including the Iranian Atomic Energy Commissioner. He said he wanted me to turn my passport over to the Navy and employ with them and leave my company. He would give me an $80,000.00 U.S. contract, a house and a car, also I would be protected by Iranian Navy. He needed me to substitute for the missing energy commissioner and to solely represent the Radiation Safety Program of all the navy's radioactive handling functions. The officers under my training were already complaining of not being paid for the past two months. So I told the commander if he would send the $80,000.00 to my U.S. account, I would consider his offer. He told me he could not do that and I would be paid once a month. I told him I'd think about the offer and left. That night a good friend of mine from England disappeared. He was employed by the Iranian Navy and was the only Rolls Royce mechanic at the ship yard. High compression, high temperature Rolls Royce engines were used in the Iranian fast patrol crafts and his billet was vitally important. A navy officer told me this Englishman hadn't been paid for over two months like all others and had lost his house and car, so a navy man had stolen his passport and the man had slipped out of Bandar Abbas aboard a British freighter during the night. I always hoped that was the truth but never knew for sure what happened.

Komeni arrived in August and began immediately clamping marshall law over all the major cities. Heads began to fly off any and all opposition from cimena owners to generals and even though his policy hadn't reached Bandar Abbas, there was a severe state of suspension on rights of movement by westerners. The British company of Wimpey was the first to leave and behind they left billions of dollars worth of heavy equipment. Brown and Root began creeping out through the

U.A.E. (United Arab Emrants) followed by Lockheed and Bell Helicopter. Many small companies remained for they simply had no way out. Iran air flights had been stopped and the airport closed leaving only the possibility of catching a freighter but tug captains wanted $2,000.00 per person to smuggle you out of the harbor.

When I returned to my room one evening and saw the machine gun nest mounted to the top of my quarters I knew it was time for me to do some heavy thinking. I could still leave camp but wasn't allowed to go into town so I took Sam and headed over the filthy beach once more. I wanted to walk and think of my future and what would happen to Sam. I knew he couldn't survive with the wild dogs and it seemed wrong that I had kept him in the first place. At the main road he sat behind the bush as always until I checked the traffic and when I said, "Hurry, Sam" he beat me across by an entire road width. While walking the beach I decided I would try getting a plane ticket out of Iran by using an American Express credit card on the black market. Maybe I could get some help from the Naval officers and possibly they could help me get rid of the two isotopes before the National Armies came. I squatted facing the Gulf to pick up some very small bright colored shells and suddenly Sam was standing by my left side. He was facing my rear will all his teeth shining and the hair standing across his back. Sam had grown to be a large heavy dog and was in the best physical shape and by his stance and low growl, I knew I should turn around very slowly. Directly behind me and about twenty five feet away, stood a huge brown dog. He was much older than Sam and the scars on him, told of many battles for survival. His body was rigid and pointing up the beach line but in his big head I could see both eyes protruding out and looking at Sam and me. I stood up very slowly and eased toward the water without looking back. I knew Sam would take the load until I got deep enough in the water to defend myself. When I was out to knee deep, I turned and whispered to Sam. He eased sideways into the water and stood alongside. Then, I saw a movement behind the huge male and noticed a large group of dogs lying flat on the beach. We were all motionless for about five minutes and there was nothing or no one in any direction as far as I could see. The huge male was the first to move, he dropped his head slightly and all the other dogs rose. They walked slowly and I counted 16 dogs following about 20 feet behind the lead dog. All of these were as large or larger than Sam. I waited until the dogs were small dots far up the beach then Sam and I lit out for the camp. About half way back to the road, Sam stopped and looked back, I couldn't see anything at first, so I told him to come on, but when he stopped the second time I looked closer and there was a young female dog sliding on her belly behind us. She was the same color as the desert and very hard to see, except when she moved. She followed us to the road, but didn't cross.

Back in camp I realized there were only sixty seven of our men left out of nearly three hundred and they had been getting out or disappearing to someplace. I think some of them had gotten out with Brown and Root, but no one was talking and since we had lost contact with Tehran, everyone was on his own. I got my passport and American Express card ready and packed some clothing to carry by hand, but for the next month everything was deathly quiet except for the terrible sounding thunder under the ground.

When Komeni's army arrived at Bandar Abbas, they casually took everything over and since they were buddies with the Navy, it seemed as though there wasn't going to be any problems. However, in about two weeks you could see groups of people gathering. All the Pakistanis and Afghans had disappeared again and civil disorder was erupting all around. Also, the army was getting into conflict with the navy and suddenly they were at my door. The two soldiers were polite, but got mad when they saw Sam, so I put him outside in his pen. They tagged my refrigerator, stove, radio, T.V., bed, table, and chairs and gave me a receipt along with a paper written in English of instructions not to remove any tagged items. I agreed and they left. The following morning I gave my passport and American Express card to an Iranian naval officer and he went into Bandar Abbas. He returned that afternoon with an exit visa and my tickets out of Iran. The receipt to American Express showed two one way tickets instead of one, so it cost me twice the fares but at this time it didn't matter, I was just glad I had the card with me. That night the officer went with me into the desert and buried the two radioactive isotopes locked inside their cameras. Then we threw the keys into the Gulf. When I returned to camp I couldn't find Sam and all night I listened for him to scratch at the door. Someone had let him out or I had forgotten to latch the door on his cage in the morning before leaving for work. As I opened my door the next morning I turned quickly and almost fainted. Sam was hanging from a beam outside my door by the neck, looped in a Texas style hangman's noose. I was sick as I ran through my room gathering the few things I would leave with. I walked past Sam without looking again and when I arrived at the ship yard the officer assigned to assist me was waiting. He already knew what had happened but couldn't talk to me about it. He rushed me to the airport at Bandar Abbas and into a room where I waited alone for the three hours. Finally he came for me and we hurried onto a plane which was loaded with Pakistanis. Upon arrival at Tehran we were met by a soldier who carried us to a concrete block room in the city. The soldier left us at 10 p.m. and returned for us at 3 a.m. the next morning. He carried us to the International airport and escorted me to the counter of Pan Am's last flight from Tehran. The man behind the counter checked my passport and ticket, then handed me a note written in English. The words were for me to pay $860.00 U.S. dollars, airport tax. I handed the note to the naval officer and told him I would not pay the money. A soldier standing nearby understood me and raised his machine gun so I began shelling out most of my last U.S. dollars. After paying, I had $50.00 left in U.S. money. I bid farewell to the officer and passed through emigrations into the final waiting area. Every place was heavily guarded and when I boarded the Pan Am flight 002 at 7 a.m., I felt sure I was free. Four hours later and no movement made me begin to feel different. According to the pilot, the Iranians had refused to load the aircraft and he had gotten it loaded by other means. Now the Iranians wouldn't allow the plane to leave until Pan Am paid them a fair loading labor fee. About an hour later the huge gray Pan Am 747 SP roared out over the ramp, taxing rapidly to the runway edge and instead of stopping as aircraft always do, the plane made a sharp right turn and buried all it's passengers in their seats with an immediate forward thrust and roar over and beyond the thunder from underneath that God forsaken land. Thirty five hours later I called my mother from Atlanta, Georgia and for once in my life I couldn't even speak. Believe it or not, I was happy to be home.

"KIDDO"

Kiddo was born on Thanksgiving Day at the home of a nice lady in North Georgia. His father was a registered Dachshund named Rusty and his mother was registered under the name of Lady. He was given to me at the age of six weeks as payment for my purchase of his mother for breeding purposes. He wasn't keen on housebreaking and hated the outside world at first. His father was very obedient and had good manners, but Kiddo had taken after his mother who was stubborn, conceited and hypo-energetic.

He traveled with me to Alabama to live temporarily in a trailer home where he found cats outside to be unbearable. He wasn't big enough to protect his food or to fight them off so he learned how to bark. This proved only to be irritating to the neighbors and meant nothing to the cats. My attempt to find work took us back through Georgia, South Carolina and eventually ended at Doctors Inlet, in Florida. There I leased a fish camp on Doctors lake near the St. John's River and purchased a small camper to live in. The winter nights were very cold along the waters edge and although I had a small electric heater, the power would constantly fail during the nights. By bundling up close with Kiddo we could keep each other warm and survival was easier.

By early spring Kiddo had grown to be a fine pup while eating a fish and bread diet with me. I moved my trailer home from Alabama to a park near the fish camp and sold the small camper. Living conditions were better for me, but Kiddo refused to stay away from the fish camp grounds, so I made him a place to sleep inside the small store. He loved this setup because if someone tried to enter the little store in my absence he wouldn't allow this and would let the whole world know about it.

I placed a picnic table outside the small store and we ate all our meals on it. Kiddo always sat at the far end of the table and waited for me to finish. When told, he would eat his meal from my plate. At any time another dog came into his area of the camp, Kiddo would get on the table to equalize his height and insist that the intruder leave. On one occasion a large black dog tried his patience and he leaped from the table locking his teeth firmly in the big dogs upper lip. The larger dog ran shaking and tumbling across the camp ground for about 100 feet. When Kiddo finally released his hold he scampered back onto the table and set himself up for the second attack, but the big dog wanted no more of this and left the camp. He was a lover of children and would readily go to their talking and laughter. He crossed the busy road in back of the little store and sat in the grass watching some children while they fished. I brought him back and whipped him gently with a newspaper, then I tied him outside the door with a large rope. He lay in the warm sand and went to sleep only to have a lady drive up and stop her car on his tail. By the time I got her to back the car away, he had almost chewed her tire off and I think he tried to tell me it was unfair to tie him like that by the way he looked at me. I crossed the busy road each day and picked up the camp mail so this gave me the opportunity to teach him not to get in the road and after a time he would sit and wait for me or sit and watch children on the other side. His favorite place on the camp was a small grassy bank just behind the store and anytime I wanted him I would find him there. I could also find shower shoes, dollar bills and most any article, which was reported lost about the camp, neatly stashed away on this little grassy slope. At one time, I found a pair of panties and a size "C" bra placed there as if they had been spread out to dry in the sun.

I began assembling trot lines at the table while waiting for customers to show and carelessly dropped one spool of cord which rolled down the bank and into the lake. Since Kiddo would sit and watch me tie these lines I figured he would play with this cord when he chased it into the water, however he brought it directly to me and laid it back on the table. I started throwing his leather bone into the lake and each time he would retrieve it. Since the bone wouldn't float he would take a deep breath and dive and search, sometimes staying down over one minute before surfacing with the bone. I continued this play with him for several days in deeper water and about the time I thought he was a real good show, I spotted the two eyes and nose tip of a large gator. He had also been observing this exercise and I knew gators love doggy for a meal. Kiddo also was aware of the fact and showed him lots of respect by leaving the area swiftly. I kept Kiddo away from the water for several days and finally the gator went on to look for a meal elsewhere.

After the lake waters warmed in the spring time, I took the trot lines and placed them in predetermined locations about the lake. Each chance I had away from the store during the week days, I would tend the lines and remove the catfish for sale to the camp owner. Kiddo always went with me on these trips and would ride on the bow when moving fast through the water. His long ears would flap in motion as if he were flying. While tending the lines he would watch attentively and the day he met his first sea cow, he almost had a heart attack. She surfaced and scratched her side on the boat then she would stick her awful ugly face out of the water and watch Kiddo frantically jump up and down in the boat. Some times she would place one flipper over my trot line and not let me lift it from the water and each trip we made to the lines she always appeared to watch Kiddo dance and bark. Once back to shore Kiddo normally wasn't the first out of the boat. He loved his trips on the lake and wouldn't take a chance of getting left behind, so I would usually have to call him to indicate we weren't going back out anytime soon.

Around this time of spring a man and his wife came to the fish camp and brought their miniature poodle named Sambo. This poodle wasn't a total stranger to Kiddo since they had met during the winter when Kiddo was very small and Sambo was already full grown at the time. On that occasion Sambo had tried to stick his thing in Kiddo's ear, eye, nose or any other hole he could find and I had reminded the lady of her dogs disrespect for Kiddo, since they were both males. She had only replied, "Oh, that is just Sambo's way of letting Kiddo know what life is all about," and she just thought it was funny. Shortly after they arrived this time, she called out, "John, stop that dog, look what he's doing to Sambo!" I followed her husband out of the little store and this time Kiddo had Sambo down and was trying to stick his thing in places where it didn't belong. I reminded the lady of the lessons Sambo taught Kiddo and if she didn't like what he was doing, she could take her Sambo and leave. I lost a customer, but protected the credibility of Kiddo. Not long after Kiddo's game with Sambo, he came up missing. I called and searched into the night, because he had never been far out of my sight and he was always in his bed at the store by 8 p.m. I thought of the gator, but hadn't seen him around in weeks. I asked the camp residents who knew Kiddo and no one had seen him. On the following day I continued my search but no Kiddo was found. He always came to a certain whistling sound but now I got no response. On the second night of missing a neighbor came by and said he had seem Kiddo near a camper which had recently arrived with New York plates. The camper was located on a rented spot near the fish camp restaurant and I found Kiddo sitting under the steps. I carried him to his bed, because he wouldn't follow me and when I locked him in the store the only thing I could figure was he had gotten mad at me for some reason and had decided to leave home. The following day he stayed with me for a while but disappeared again when I wasn't looking. I found him again at the steps of the new arrivals. A lady answered the door and after I explained my problem she told me her little poodle was in heat. I took Kiddo to my trailer and got a large white onion. I split it in half and rubbed it all over his nose, head and ears. I took him back to the fish camp and placed him in his bed and he slept for three days. When he finally woke up, the people with the poodle had moved on, so he was himself again.

One morning during Kiddo's eighth month of life, I unlocked the store door and he shot by me and ran through the early morning darkness toward the camp restaurant. This was unusual, since he always greeted me with kisses all over for at least five minutes. As I proceeded to unlock the gas pump and secure the pier lights, I could hear him barking in a panic from underneath a vehicle parked near the side of the restaurant. It wasn't unusual for someone to leave their car there overnight and I thought at first it might be a cat. The alternate whine or whimper between barks was unusual to Kiddo's normal growl, so I went around the car to get a look. Lying there on his back was the old man who raked leaves and cleaned the camp ground for the owner. Getting closer I could see bubbles rising from the saliva in his mouth and realized he had fell from a heart attack. I wanted to attempt to get his heart stated again, but I didn't know anything about this man and also realized only Kiddo would be my witness. I ran to the pay phone and called the rescue unit, then returned to the man. Whatever had happened wasn't violent since the rake had been slowly drown across his chest, his hand still gripping it. Four minutes later the rescue team arrived and the owner of the camp arrived directly behind them. The man was pronounced dead and I told the owner I may have been able to save him. The owner told me if I had hit him in the chest without a witness present I would have been sued by his sister who was a very mean ornery and stupid person. Even for just finding him there, I was questioned for two hours by her attorney and the coroner. Not long after this Kiddo pulled a similar stunt only this time he was by the Dempsey dumpster and I just refused to investigate. I could visualize a body in that dumpster and how on Earth would I explain it. After the owner arrived we walked together to the dumpster and looking out over the side was a cat, twice the size of Kiddo. He jumped out and as Kiddo chased him across the camp ground I could hear his big feet slapping against the protruding roots. He must have thought he was the greatest hero of all to put a cat that size in flight. Even after the cat cleared the north camp fence, I heard Kiddo give him a couple of good barks and a fierce growl.

September arrived and bream in Doctors Lake began to bed. I waited until the females had left the beds, then took Kiddo in the boat to look for good locations. The water is warm and the best way to catch bream from the beds is to wade. I anchored my boat outside the tall grass and left Kiddo to guard it. While wading, I wouldn't always be in view of the boat, but Kiddo would bark at anyone who came near or tried to steal it. I left my billfold on the boat seat and waded into the thick grass. I returned two hours later, after locating two large bream beds and had caught sixteen, weighing a quarter pound each. Kiddo greeted me with several kisses and when I looked into the boat I couldn't believe my eyes. He had removed every item from my billfold, including money and had placed it neatly throughout the boat. He hadn't torn or damaged anything, but had positioned each card, picture, license, identification and money from bow to stern, as if creating some sort of game. He assisted me in gathering it all up and was very helpful as if this was another part of the game. The following day I returned to this same spot and this time along with Kiddo, I brought a fishing friend. When I raised the motor and placed my billfold on top of it out of Kiddo's reach, I told him what had happened the previous day. He said, he never carried his on him when he went wade fishing, so we left the boat and left Kiddo on guard. After one hour we had caught thirty one large bream between the two of us but a dark cloud was approaching rapidly from the west. We began hurrying back to the boat through waist deep water. When we reached the boat the high winds preceeding the rain had swept it into the deep grass. Once in the boat we both pushed our way out of the grass and I dropped the motor in the water. Kiddo disappeared under the seats as the bottom fell out of that cloud and we raced for the landing. As I turned the boat to beach it at the fish camp, I thought of my billfold. A search after the storm turned up nothing and although I was able to replace my license and identification, I could never replace the valuable photos and certifications. I wished I had let Kiddo play his game, at least I would still have the pieces.

Thanksgiving Day arrived and I cooked a small turkey. I planned to take the afternoon off and watch the games on T.V., so Kiddo came to the trailer with me. I gave him an entire drumstick from the turkey and wished him a happy first birthday, then put him outside with the leg. A few minutes later I heard another dog run past the trailer barking and heard Kiddo come from under the trailer barking and taking chase. Suddenly, I heard car tires scream on the pavement at the main road and almost immediately a girl from one of the trailers nearby, came running to my door crying. She said, "Kiddo's been hit!" I ran from the trailer to the highway and he was lying alongside in the grass. As I lifted him up I knew he was dying. His lungs were filling rapidly with blood and his left eye had been knocked out of his head. A neighbor ran to his car and returned begging me to carry him to the animal hospital. The children which the other dogs were barking at were crying and said they had yelled for Kiddo to go back. They had been across the road and saw the car dodge the large red dog but it hit Kiddo. I held him and talked to him about going fishing in the boat until his heart stopped. He was very strong and young with a full healthy life ahead, if he had lived, but the one mistake of chasing that dog had ruined both our Thanksgiving Day festivities. I walked slowly back to my trailer with Kiddo in my arms as the neighbors watched. Once inside I wrapped him in a clean sheet and carried him to the little grassy slope in back of the fish camp store. There I dug his grave and buried him on his first birthday. When I turned away to return to my trailer the red dog stood looking at me. I took out the loaded pistol which I always carried in my back pocket and I pointed at the dogs head. I said, "You are to blame for Kiddo's death", then I saw two men standing near the water looking at me. They knew what had happened and I thought, maybe, this dog meant as much to someone as Kiddo had meant to me, I doubt it, but just maybe. There's one thing for sure, Kiddo didn't finish eating his Thanksgiving dinner and neither did I.

"THE IMPOSSIBLE DREAM"

Every man working away from his home and family for long lengths of time, regardless of what country, must accept the challenge to specific facts which govern the moral and mental capabilities of husband and wife. Men are drawn to developing countries primarily for money and in every case, he has high hopes of achieving specific goals within a certain time frame. Depending upon placement some reach their desired limits ahead of schedule and others are required to stay abroad longer. Very few cases exist where the reasons are through greed because a greedy man does not perform to the standards of the man in need. The principals of the married man lie within the bounds of his self-discipline and ability to foresee destiny. Faith in our all-mighty God is a must if there is to be any contentment with himself during his long sleepless nights. Moral aptitude drops rapidly and impotence threatens. He may develop a fear of his opposite sex through lack of mental stimulation. His loss of responsibility with his household will no doubt cause conflict upon return and tends to break him down as the man of the past. As time passes to him, his friends and personal contacts back home diminish. The only consolation a man working abroad has is his job, his rest and his previously set goals. Men working in the far east have some chance with many opportunities to stray from their codes of conduct and moral beliefs. However, for those working in middle east Islamic countries the crooked path does not exist. Here, the mans beliefs must not be disclosed. On a daily basis, he must face the baron world of dust, heat, security police, head on collisions, lack of communications and fear of breaking the law within a custom he does not understand. For example, the carrying of a picture of your wife in a bathing suit can draw you a two year jail sentence. When we speak of loosing your head, this can be used in literal terms, if a man attempts to communicate in any way with an Islamic woman His chances of getting into trouble are great, but would not be through social or moral misconduct. These along with drugs or alcohol in any fashion, are sure death.

Statistics show the married man working abroad stands very little chance of holding his family together without a firm permanent belief between he and his wife toward specific goals in life. The unmarried man does not necessarily set goals and seldom saves his money, but the married man may send back all except a small amount, kept for his survival. Of all the men working in Middle East Islamic countries, 40 percent will be divorced within two to five years. A break down shows only 3 percent divorced in the age range of 50 years and 70 years, 12 percent between the ages of 20 years and 35 years, but 25 percent between the age of 35 years to 50 years. The older seem to be more stable, probably due to their inability to get work back home and long term marriages seeking retirement. The younger group appear to be getting a start in life and are more prone to achieve these goals together. The middle group tend to run into problems with moral and social activities generating from life's changes and fears of growing old without a feeling of full physical and mental life time achievement.

For the married woman who has a husband working abroad, the daily life burdens are four times greater. She must now accept the total responsibility of rearing the children, maintaining the household and face all the financial problems which arise through bills, taxes, insurance and maintenance. Her job at home alone is far more taxing on her mental and emotional capabilities than those of her husband. Her chances of getting into trouble are ten fold compared to his because she must maintain a social atmosphere to avoid going insane. She cannot fit into a single group because of her marriage and cannot fit into the married functions because she has no husband. Her nerves become shattered and she resorts to doctor's advise with prescriptions which ease her mental and physical needs on a temporary basis, but causes her to require more and more drugs to face life alone. She may begin to chain smoke or drink alcohol which decreases her mental capability to cope with the coming days and her health will begin to diminish through emotional exhaustion. As she returns to the same empty house, there is no welcome, no love or reassurance, no one to tell her the nice things she needs to hear or join with her in laughter, and the desire to go on isn't there anymore. She may attempt to boast her ego in an attempt to fight off the fear of total boredom, by eliminating her friends or making daring attempts to prove to herself that better days are ahead by drawing attention or making a scene, but deep in her heart she knows it must end and this mental anguish must stop. She may have inexperienced council to turn to and she will be ill advised by these sources.

When we attempt to relate out thoughts toward the proper things to do, we may only come up with a few. Each case would seem to be different but the ground rules are almost always identical. For the husband considering prospective employment abroad, two major factors must be thoroughly analyzed. Have the common goals desired by the husband been thoroughly digested by the wife's mind and if so, can these be achieved with the respect and loyalty over the time frame allotted? If the wife does not agree with the needs of money or the husband's goals, she may feel that love and security are of more importance, however, we all know no one will hand you a living on a silver platter and life itself is a struggle bound with self sacrifice. If you are a married man and you believe you can work away from home and achieve the goals of home, transportation, recreation, investment and retirement without your wife's full consent, then you believe in the impossible dream.

"THE FIRST AND LAST TIME"

When I arrived at Mobile, from my job in Saudi Arabia, I had prepared a list of "must do" items on a priority basis. First, call your $3,500.00 attorney and find out what he had accomplished toward your divorce suit. Next, rent a car, then go find a motel. Afterwards shop around for some decent clothing especially buy a suit for your court appearance. Most all things in between the major items could be accomplished as they occurred. Being adrift in mind from 25 hours of flying and a 9 hour time change, doesn't help matters when a person needs to concentrate on ways to prevent loosing 3 years of his life in the desert with no one to talk with except himself. Chances were, I would be able to get everything back since she had deserted me over 5 months ago, but of course this was just hopeful thinking.

A call to my attorney drained the remaining strength from my body as this over paid mouth piece began filling me in on the results of his less than zero efforts in my case. My wife had counter sued for a $187,000.00 cash and property settlement charging mental cruelty since I had spent 97 days with her in our 3 years of marriage. He advised me to get out of town and don't talk to anyone about the case. I was to call him back when I landed in a safe, far away place and he would give me the trial date.

I rented a $47.00 per day car from Avis and went looking for a place to lay my head down. I checked into a downtown motor court and tried to get some rest but this was next to impossible. My mind was so cluttered with things I needed to get done and my thoughts were just short of killing certain people. I wanted to be alone but once alone I couldn't stand myself for being such a fool in the first place. I managed to make it through the night between nightmares and deep thought. I hadn't felt like eating anything since I was staring at a daily motel bill of $35.00 minimum with any decency and along with the rent-a-car There would be gas and food to buy plus I still needed some clothes. I decided to drive to North Georgia where I was always welcome at my mothers home. At least I could work for my keep and would stay out of trouble with my wife's people or her and the law.

When I arrived at the check out desk I noticed a young girl sitting alone in the lounge. She was very pretty and she smiled pleasantly as I said, "Good morning." As I paid my bill I thought I should not have said anything to her since I could feel her eyes on each side of my spinal cord. When I thanked the clerk and turned, she stood up. Now being a red blooded, physically fit, desert tanned male, I couldn't hold back certain green thoughts. To top all else, I hadn't seen my wife or been near a woman in 9 months and I wasn't liable to be holier than thou if this girl did make her approach. Almost if rehearsed the show was on. She smiled shyly and addressed me as "Stranger", reminded me of a country and western song I had heard and of course I smiled back and mannerly gave her the "Yes, mam". She asked where I was headed and my thoughts instantly bounced off to where was she headed, because it didn't really matter to me, but I concentrated on my conscience to guide me and I told her I was going to Georgia. She wondered if I could please give her a lift to Montgomery and even if it had been out of my way, I would have obliged.

We didn't talk much as we entered the car and she wasn't used to the run of mill women's lib treatment, such as hold her dainty little hand as she entered the car, tuck her in snugly and safely, lock and close her door. No, she didn't really care for all this, she just wanted a bottle of scotch, some ice, a glass, a pizza pie and carry her by a friend's house before leaving town. I knew if one of my wife's kin-folk or friends recognized me with her in the car before I got out of Mobile it would be curtains for me but what the heck this might be worth it and I was about fed up with being the only innocent husband in town anyway. I figured I'd let her have her way until we got out of town then I could be the boss, so I carried her to a housing project on the south side. She returned after about five minutes and asked if she could borrow $30.00 from me to pay her girl friend a debt for her food during a visit. I had a twenty and a five, so I let her borrow the latter amount, because it made her very happy and she said, "Love, I'll be right back to you". Boy, I tell you the steam was just sizzling off my body, her making remarks like that to me. I could visualize a beautiful trip to Montgomery and a wonderful relationship in the making. This was going to be my day and I wished I had gotten some rest last night. I was about to figure this may be a Jamaican watch sale deal, when she finally came out of the apartment after thirty five minutes. I wasn't really interested in what took so long, since she was returning and what the heck, time was the worst enemy I was facing at present. Well, I thought it was anyway. She had gotten some ice and two glasses from her friend and we were off. A quick stop at the state liquor store and pizza parlor would be nothing now, because I would handle that. I picked up two fifths of scotch and two fifths of Canadian Mist, so we would be on the safe side and grabbed a pizza on the next block. When I arrived with the pizza, she had already mixed us a drink on the rocks and I noticed her nose was a red fire. She had a slight tan and a real pretty face, but this nose stood out like a rag weed, so I asked about it being that way. "Oh", she said, " I have this awful nose itch when I'm excited and I rub my nose very hard". I told her she shouldn't do that anymore, cause it might fall off. Before we had reached the interstate 65 North, she had let me know what she thought of my choice in low tense country music and had one of those stations tuned in with space music, so loud the windshield wipers were vibrating. Each time I turned it down she turned it back up. I knew when she got a couple of shots of that scotch down, she would go to sleep then I could give my ear drums a break, so I let them suffer for the time being. It didn't happen that way, but suddenly she yelled, "Stop the car, stop the car!" I pulled over to the emergency stop lane and she jumped out vomiting and rubbing her nose. I turned that confounded noise off and asked her what was wrong but she wouldn't say anything. She got back into the car slowly and I asked if she had any breakfast. Her reply was no, so I tried to give her a piece of pizza. She refused, saying "I'll eat some of it later." When she said she was O.K. we traveled on north, me sipping on my Canadian Mist and her guzzling down scotch and bursting my ear drums with that loud noise on the radio. By the time we reached the first exit with a gas station on it, I was in extreme need for a rest room and I'm sure she was also. I hadn't had a chance to talk with the girl, because of that music and I made my mind up to lessen the racket or put her out. I didn't even know her name, but to think of it she hadn't asked me mine either. When we got back on the road I told her the noise level would have to be much lower and she didn't disagree with me, so we began to chat. She was holding her scotch really well, but my tongue was beginning to get in the way and slurred my voice. She said she was 23 years old and had worked as a registered nurse in Birmingham. I couldn't believe she was a registered nurse at 23, but wasn't in any mood to make waves. I told her about my job in Saudi Arabia and about my divorce pending, etc., etc. She liked the idea of us getting better acquainted and began to make plans for her own apartment, car and income. She said her mother and father were having hard times making ends meet and she wasn't helping by having to get money from them. The hospital fired her for getting too many phone calls, so she said.

I realized I was getting about drunk and I couldn't remember my last meal, so I suggested we stop some place and rest for a few hours, get some food and travel on later in the day, but she wouldn't have any part of the idea. This irked me, because I was beginning to see my plan failing at my own expense and it reminded me of the times I had felt left out before. I knew I didn't have to tell her what I was thinking because she looked over at me and said you will just have to wait till we get there. I asked, "When we get where?", and she said she wanted me to take her to Birmingham, because that's where her mother and father lived.

By the time we reached Montgomery the girl's nose had about regained its color, but she had drank almost two thirds of the first bottle of scotch. I was about crocked on my Canadian Mist and had decided to go into Birmingham, then take Interstate 20 west to Atlanta. We made four more rest room stops between Montgomery and Birmingham and she finished off the first bottle of scotch. She pointed out the way for me to arrive at a motel just inside the city limits and I don't even know the name of it. I never even knew the girl opened the second bottle of scotch and wouldn't have believed she was able to do it anyway. I couldn't see the register, so I scribbled an alias name and address across the card. Apparently it was acceptable because they gave me a key and the girl assisted me from the car to the room. I carried a cold pizza pie and my shoulder bag, while she brought the ice bucket, drink bottles and her hand bag.

Once inside the door I began trying to sober up by splashing water over my face, she was on the telephone. As soon as she hung up, she said we had to make a trip and I explained to her I was in no shape to drive. She said she would drive and knew the way, plus she knew the cops if we should get stopped. I wouldn't go, but by now she had the car keys and was out the door.

When she headed down back streets at a high rate of speed, I reminded her what I had brought her to Birmingham for and demanded she take me back to the motel and pay off. She promised me she would as soon as we got back. I wasn't sober enough to watch the road, so I just relaxed and hung on. She pulled into a deserted diner parking area and picked up a black man, who said he had been out of luck and pointed out the directions for her to drive on. I managed to strike up a conversation with the man but had no idea what was going on. Along the way she became frantic with impatience in traffic and I got scared. This seemed to be restoring what little brain I had left to function and I started making my plan to escape if they both got out of the car. I thought the devil with my bag at the motel but where on earth was I? I knew the police would get me for sure if I got lost in my condition and I definitely was lost.

We arrived in what looked like executive housing, and the black man got out and disappeared into the darkness. I said, "What the hell's going on?", and she told me to hush, keep quiet and give her $180.00. I said, "Like hell I will", and she began jerking the car in first gear, then reverse, making the tires scream forward and backwards. She said, "Give me the money and I'll give you anything you want, when we get back to the motel." I asked her when would that be and what was the money for? She said to never mind about what it was for and we would return directly to the motel. I fumbled around and got the money out, she took it, got out of the car and impatiently paced up and down the street. I looked for the keys but she wasn't stupid, she had them in her hand. I searched through her hand bag for a gun, I planned to use it if necessary to make my escape. There wasn't anything in there which felt like a gun but I found the equipment for giving injections and my stupid brain began to draw a picture. I figured she won't let any harm come to me as long as I play along and say the things she wants to hear, then when the chance arises, I'll split with the wind.

The girl jumped into the car sharply just as the black man appeared in the street light and suddenly he was in the back seat. He handed her a small brown envelope and she gave him the money. She said, "Six", and he said, "Yep". The trip back through those back streets was just as hazardous as before, but there was no need to worry, if its your time to go, you're going to go anyway. The black man asked me how long I'd known the girl and I told him for a long time. He said, "Man she is mean now when she gets on it", then turned and asked her if she had settled down any. She told him she had never been mean and I told him I agreed with her, also that she and I were planning a good future and she was moving to her own apartment. Her eyes lit up like street lights and a big smile came over her face as she began telling the black man about the car she was going to get and her income would allow her to live decent for a change. I knew all would be o.k. for me now and there wouldn't be any trouble for me, so if I could get back to the motel, I would sneak out when she went to the bathroom. She dropped the black man off at the deserted diner and continued to tell me about our future plans as she sped toward the motel. When we arrived I had sobered some and got about good on my own now but I was weak. I had no idea what time it was since I couldn't see my watch plainly. But it was either five minutes past ten or ten minutes till one. I knew it had been dark for a long time.

Inside the motel room the girl immediately took out the equipment from her hand bag. She removed the needle from the syringe and placed them on the dresser. She took six small pink pills out of the brown envelope and explained the dosage to me. I told her I wasn't interested, I had never done anything like that, never tasted the stuff or used it and wasn't planning to start now. I told her I'm 50 years old and lived a healthy life without it and she was only 23 years old and already it was ruining her life. I told her how pretty she was without it and now I knew why her nose was so red and she was sick when she left Mobile. Also this answered the question of why she didn't get drunk from drinking an entire bottle of scotch. I told her it was no wonder her parents couldn't afford her and she was jobless. She was amused at my lecture and paid no mind as she hastened to prepare this dose of whatever it was. She placed two of the small pills between a folded piece of paper and began popping her teeth together across the paper which caused the pills to crush inside. As she poured the powder into the syringe she explained my dose would only be one pill, since it was my first time. I again told her I didn't need any pill, I'm drunk enough as it is. She then promised to give me some loving and it would make me last a long time. She said my mind would be clear and I would feel good all over and I would have a wonderful time. At my age I figured I might need some help so I agreed to take half of one pill. She explained that wouldn't do me any good, because I was a grown man and believe her, she knew the dosage because she had been a registered nurse. She placed the syringe under the spigot and drew a small amount of warm water into the powder, then placed the needle over the end and shook the syringe briskly. The powder turned to a light pink solution and she said it was ready, so she removed a small leather strap from her hand bag and wrapped it around her arm. Squeezing tight, she held the strap in her teeth and injected the liquid into her vein on top of her hand as she loosened the small strap. She then cleaned the syringe and started to crush the pill for me. I told her I wasn't using a used syringe and she got out a new one from her pack. She processed the pill in the same manner as before and when she had it ready, I had changed my mind. Again, I wanted her to go to the bathroom so I could escape and I knew if I had good sense I'd walk out anyway. She took out a clipping from a newspaper and asked me to read it. I did and it was about some members of congress walking out of a session on a certain date in argument over a certain bill and the bill failed by so many votes. After I read the clipping she said she would ask me some questions about what I had read to test my awareness. Hell, I hadn't paid any attention to the thing in preparation for a test and it must have been years ago when it happened. I answered the questions she asked, then she read the answer back to me correctly and compared my answer. Out of five, I missed four, but not entirely just not exactly. She said the pill would make me fully aware and my senses would work wonders for me. It sounded interesting, but I told her if it was that good and since she had taken hers, would she mind passing a test for me. She agreed, so I took out a pack of camel cigarettes and told her to read the sentence on back of the pack. She had thirty seconds to look, then tell me how many e's small and capital inclusive, that she saw. Never had anyone got this correct on their first try and I've been smoking camels for thirty five years. When her thirty seconds were up, I pulled the pack away and she answered eleven. I told her that was a wild guess and for her to guess again. She said there's eleven and told me where they were and what the sentence said. She then swore she had never seen the sentence before, so I agreed to take the pill and we could get on with the chores at hand. I wouldn't take it any place except in the large vein at my elbow and she strapped my arm an had me hold the strap.

Shortly afterwards, I felt like I had been given an I.V. for kidney stones and began feeling very sick to my stomach. I jumped up to run into the bathroom and fell over the opposite bed. Once in the bathroom I vomited but nothing came up. I was deathly sick now and scared because I knew there was no antidote for what was in my blood stream. I wobbled back into the room and fell on the bed. As I lay there looking up the room began to turn and when I closed my eyes the ball continued to turn in its socket. I yelled at her for giving me this mess and told her it might kill me. She said, lay there and relax you will feel much better in a few minutes. By now she had started rubbing her nose again and it had started turning red. I wondered how long it would take for mine to do the same but right now I was trying to figure out why I was so very sick at my stomach and my chest was burning. I tried to raise myself off the bed and I couldn't get up, I couldn't even turn my body over on my side. The room was quiet and the girl was looking at herself in the dresser mirror, sitting there appearing as a statue to me, without making a move or sound. I fell suddenly into a deep sleep and when I awoke I thought I was in a combat zone. I was still on my back fully clothed and there was shattered glass all over my body and the bed. The first thing I saw was the huge mirror missing from the dresser. That girl had thrown something through it and it shattered all over the room. All the covers had been ripped off the other bed and the table lamps were on the floor with the bulbs still lighted. The water was running in the bathroom and that girl was throwing the towels and trash basket out. I jumped off the bed, grabbed my bag and ran through the door. I found the car and I sped away from the motel not knowing which direction to turn. After about two blocks I saw a sign which said Interstate 65 North and I was lucky, because in less than a mile another sign said Interstate 20 East, exit one mile. I looked at the clock in the car and it was 3:15 a.m., so I have no idea how long I was asleep or whatever I was. I do know the police had to be on their way to the motel because there was no way that much noise could go unreported. The fact was, I had to get away from there without getting caught, my divorce was in progress in Mobile and this would have been definite news to hang me with down there. I had registered under a false name, was under the influence of some kind of drug, almost total destruction of the room had to be answered for and that girl still had three more of those pills if she didn't take them while I was asleep. Needless to say, that was my first time in 50 years and the last time in the next 50 years that I will ever let myself get involved with any sort of dope or with anyone that associates themselves with dope.

"THIRD WORLD HARI NATAL (CHRISTMAS)"

The beautiful music began about twenty days before the event, as the spirit began to burst out of long anticipation but this died out to low key after two or three days since the days are long and this tended to break down with the loneliness of night. It may have started too soon for some but they would regain their courage to face the longing for their loved ones through the spirit being aroused by others. As the day of festivities neared within four, this new and more vigorous tempo began to come alive among all who associated themselves with another. I believe the disappearance of the spirit from the seventeenth day till the fourth day was due to an inability of relationships in shopping and sharing together, along with the virtual nonexistence of the surroundings normally associated with Christmas time. No doubt there could have been other things which caused nations of representatives inside an eighty foot by forty foot space to live and share side by side for a year on a day to day basis. One wonders what ever happened to cause conflict in the first place. Not only are these men different nationalities but they differ in customs, religion, race, color and language. Their harmony and enjoyment of each other's company is far surpassed to the every day neighborhood rapport. They readily discuss their common goals and strive hard to achieve these.

The Indonesian may be working away from home this Christmas to make enough money to start a business. Normally he is in his fifth year and needs a little more money so he can return and live peacefully in his country.

The Filipino is most definitely away from his family this year, for reasons of future security for his wife and young children. The Lebanese captain is here to make better for his family and to restore future in his war torn land. The Bahraine has come to work and improve his skills within the competitive Arab market. The Thai want more for their families and are required to support the members who are old and poor. This pertains also to the Filipino customs of living. The Sri-Lankans want to make some money to establish a business for their future. The American and British are here in an effort to achieve life time goals, of which they have previously been unsuccessful in doing. In all, there will be seven Indonesians, one Lebanese, two Sri-Lankans, three Thai, one Bahraine, seventeen Filipinos, one British and one American, spending Christmas together at sea on one small lonely ship in the Persian Gulf.

Those who have served in the Asiatic Campaigns, Third World countries and Far East can understand and appreciate this rival of customs since they readily recognize the resentment, yet inquisitive attitudes toward Eastern customs. In all cases a method of positive proof must be available before one gets himself involved in a show and tell session. These men observe the very existence of every Western influence and are continuously aware of your moves, both day and night. They will taste and give comment to anything which a Westerner may associate himself with or assist in preparing. If it is good to his taste you won't have to ask for a comment. He will show his true feelings and no matter how complicated the mix or recipe was to perform, you won't have to show him a second time. He will always serve it to you later, exactly as you have demonstrated in your single performance. When we think of a grilled cheese we think of next to nothing to preparation. Ironically when fixed correctly this sandwich can be very delicious to taste. My introduction of the grilled cheese was accepted by the Thai cook after careful preparation and is now used for combating sea sickness during heavy seas. Prior to the demonstration packs of cheese were only left to develop freezer burn and be discarded. One of my biggest problems was to get a roast duck on the menu. Somehow, these ducks had been shipped in as turkey and Third World people have no trouble accepting turkey or chicken but a duck prepared like chicken isn't very appealing to them. At first they were confused and required encouragement but when we roasted the duck, its taste appealed and they accepted.

One of the careful areas of discussion is politics. Care must be taken to address the favorable portions and know the specific countries to talk about. In other words, make sure you aren't making a comment related to the political situation in Indonesia, if a Filipino has asked the question. Some favorite criticism can be aimed at Communism or terroristic activities since most all of these people have been subjected to this way of life at one time or another. In most all cases this will draw a conversation about previous experiences from those who can speak partial English and they will interpret for those who can't.

A subject from West to Far East must always be avoided concerning religion. Usually, you are unaware of the presence of Hindu, Muslims, Buddha and Christian beliefs within a small group of friendly men and this very subject in any text, can prove to be most embarrassing.

The ships cook had planned to barbecue one of the three large Lapu-Lapu (American grouper fish) for Christmas dinner, but these were required for their meals in the approaching days so he is hoping the turkeys which were previously promised will arrive in time. One of the most favorite diets of the Third world people is fish and white rice. This food gives them a beautiful smooth complexion and they remain strong and slim. Less desirable are their furnished foods of chicken and beef so they will hang a line into the water at any time their work load permits in an effort to catch their favorite food.

Unfortunately the supply boat did not bring turkey on its bi-monthly trip two days before Christmas and any special meal would now be pure speculation. There was a few cans of salmon and I showed the cook how to make salmon patties. Since they like to add pet pep (an extremely hot sauce) to each meal, I always asked for a separate serving and the salmon patties were no exception. Along with the short supplies come other miseries like insufficient amounts of toilet paper, cigarettes, stamps and writing paper. Most of the men had learned to survive by having their families send letter writing supplies and they would approach anyone going ashore about bringing them some stamps, which they called stomps. Mail was considered more or less a luxury and it wasn't expected to go or come on a regular basis. One receiving a letter three months old was appreciated in the same manner as a letter which was eight days old.

Since these men have no identification for going ashore and spend their entire contract on the water, time is of no essence and in most cases current news could have been events of last year. I explained to them how they could conserve their toilet paper by using one square per man which got a lot of laughs and increased morale among them. I couldn't suggest a solution to the smoking or writing problem but promised to help any way I could.

The spirit among all remained high and it wasn't because of artificial means, since in their present location of the world spirits of that type would be totally prohibited. I can't say that no spirits were available because among all talents anything is possible but I can say it would have been illegal.

On the day before Christmas the captain had received word through his company that his daughter had sent a message by returning nationals. Her word from Lebanon was, "All is o.k., the Palestinians have gone, but Mom wants to know what is the problem?"

A man working away from his loved ones does not sleep, eat or function properly when he is worried and the captain had many responsibilities in his job and since he had not heard from his family in over two months it's enough to make a mind fold up. Sometimes a man would wonder if the same light shines in different shades of color to different minds. However his happiness was a great contribution to the crew and added to their motivation. Not all of these nationalities will openly discuss their problems and especially they won't enter into any contest of opinions about immediate family thoughts. On rare occasions one will mention or display photos of his loved ones but this is highly unusual. He reserves all rights and privileges of his family to be his concern and he accepts that full responsibility. As I would say, " I will ask my wife about something unusual", he would say, "I will see." It appears to be much simpler his way and I accept his as a firm responsible control of the situation. Not one of these men disregard their family's position in society, security, health or welfare. They readily recognize that their loved ones cannot have a normal Christmas without them and since they are also heavily burdened, it's not uncommon to see silent tears flow down their cheeks in a particular conversation. The fact that it is Christmas has no bearing in a sense, when we mingle among these different beliefs.

Ramadan or Haj could cause the same reaction, since mankind blends together in one soup of delicate friendship when the spirit of events touch them. If there is a percentage of apathetic attitudes here, it hasn't been recognized and even worse if it were, the situation would be resolved among themselves.

Christmas came and went almost uneventful from its physical aspects of tree decorations, dancing and being merry, etc., etc., but harmony of togetherness was evident to such an extent, that we received knowledge in several different ways of life, as spirit of Christmas enhanced each nationality. All of us here can readily accept that we can learn things which are further than we see and touch, that all men are created equal and no man holds the abundance of knowledge, that it isn't what we give, but how we give it and that we recognize all humans as beings with heart and soul. Names like Eddy Manurung, Norm Praikratoke, Selamat Manuari, Ferry Katuuk, Amir Lubis, Khalid Kmograbi, Yunus Bunga, Ahmed Hussin, Johnathan Borja, Renato Fenis and many others won't be remembered by me but I will remember that when our expressions and smiles display true friendship with regards to all alike, we will be rewarded through our inner feelings and if being unkind or unfriendly to these men during Christmas time would have made me appear more mature, I hope to God, I never grow up.

"JEALOUSY"

A strange human and animal characteristic, which has puzzled laymen and professionals for as long as life exists, would no doubt cause great concern. A young child who cries for its mother's attention on a continuous basis may not be hurting for other than total love and affection. Another child who cannot let its parents talk with the neighbors without making a fuss or wrecking something, probably is approaching the second stage of this terrible mental disorder which will follow him to his grave unless immediate steps are taken by his parents.

Jealousy may occur as a congenital disease or it may occur later in life as a mental disorder. In any case, it is the most dreaded characteristic of all other attitudes existing in living form. It destroys homes, jobs and even lives of the carrier. Only two causes of this terminal problem are available for study and both are delicate and sensitive. One is defined as the lack of confidence and inability to cope with the future of living. This causes a seeking of stability within the present or an attempt to recapture the past. Recognition is needed on a continuous basis and those who offer this sort of help will find themselves in a binding situation. The other cause for jealousy is the need of total love and affection. When we put the two causes together, we find a very disturbing pattern of events.

For example, a child's mother is divorced from his father and her new husband doesn't get along with the young lad. The child is taken to live with his grandfather on his mothers side of the family. He is placed in a low class school along with a niece of the same age. The young boy gets into trouble with the other boys at the school and is sent to the clinic. His grandfather goes to the higher class school board and upon recommendation of the clinic, the young lad is transferred. The niece's mother is a very jealous woman and accuses her father of being unfair to her child by not getting her daughter transferred to the higher class school also. The grandfather explaines the justification but to a jealous person there is no reasoning. Eventually, this young man becomes a hated part of the family by the jealous woman. She continually reminds her father of the neglect in her childhood and for her children. Ultimately, this leads to jealous hatred and hatred toward the jealous.

Another case is a man who met a new friend. They fished and hunted together and unknowing to his new friend, this man had a jealous friend already. When the new friend and his wife were invited over for a visit on Sunday, they had no idea it would end just short of their death. Shortly after their arrival, the jealous friend arrived and displayed an obvious resentment. Since he could not devote his total attention to his jealous friend, that one insulted the new friend in an attempt to break the friendship. Pursuing conversation led to a fight and the jealous friend was knocked to the ground by the man's new friend. The jealous man left and returned with a pistol holding both families at bay and threatening to kill everyone unless the man got rid of his new friend. The jealous man had no recognition to law of order and felt that his life was useless without the man who gave him confidence and affection. The man agreed not to see his new friend and later had to move his family to an unknown place in order to rid them of this diseased person. A jealous man can cause another to loose his job and break him down socially to the point his family will no longer respect him.

Still another case was of three men working on a ship in the Arabian Gulf. This consisted of an American Project Inspector, a British Project Management Supervisor and the ships Chief Engineer from Indonesia. The Chief Engineer liked the American inspector and was jealous of him to the extent he would not allow any of the other crew members near him. He didn't have any jurisdiction over the British supervisors functions and began to develop a hatred toward the American for their business associations. He tried to give the American gifts to win his affection and was refused. He was reminded by the American of his official status and ordered to stay within these boundaries of responsibility. This further angered the Chief, but he had no control over his jealousy and continued attempts to violate the principals of the American office. When word was received about the American inspectors departure, the Chief sat in the ships gallery crying. The American paid no attention and finished his meal. When the British supervisor approached and told the American he should be ashamed for not letting the Chief kiss him good-bye, the Chief perked up. At that, the Brit kissed the American on his bald head and said, "See that Chief, he let me kiss him good-bye". The Chief became instantly violent throwing a deck of cards across the galley, lunged over a table and grabbed the American by the neck choking and twisting his head. The American threw a glass of water at the Chief, then hit him in the head with the large glass. The American Inspector didn't sleep that night and kept his room locked for fear this jealous man would cut his throat. This disease has no limits to it's destructive powers and it's not uncommon for a jealous husband to walk into a place, see his wife dancing with another man and blow the innocent party away. A jealous woman marrying a man can't let him out of her sight long enough for him to hold down a job. She wants his lips locked on hers twenty-four hours a day and if they aren't, she believes they were locked on another woman. Normally, jealous people have no feelings of responsibility and very little comprehension. They have no use for good thoughts and these become passing feelings but they always retain the neglect of total affection toward them and use these to fuel their hatred.

There is one inevitable fact, when you have become exposed to a jealous person or animal there is the slow pattern of hatred which must always follow. If I knew a way to help such tormented minds I would no doubt be in a different job classification. But through my experience and close contact with people from all over the world, I've witnessed some things of which I truly believe did change the outlook in many peoples lives. Surely, one of these would not be to neglect a child's love and affection but where a firm foundation of respect and discipline are concerned among the young, it is a must. This doesn't mean, Mom and Dad spare the rod and grandparents pamper, this pertains to the entire family structure. They must think of the child's future and from day one this program must be thoroughly observed. Special attention might be given to allowing the child an opportunity to work out his problem. A purposely lost child in the woods will find his own way out and gain confidence that he did this himself. If he packs his bag to leave home help him and offer a sandwich but don't beg him to stay, he'll be back soon enough as it is. Give him every opportunity possible to obey instructions then offer recognition. What must be done at all cost, is to instill confidence within himself, the total need for love and affection will diminish as his confidence increases. In the older person there seems to be only one thing to do but first, you must be alert to recognize this characteristic. Once the symptoms are positive, you must be direct and firm with him. Since jealousy only has a positive or negative trait, he must either accept or reject you. Now if his decision is negative your relationship can only go on the rocks. If he is positive and sticks with this decision, he can be a good neighbor and friend.

"GO EAST YOUNG MAN"

It wouldn't be unusual to observe a large flock of Canadian Geese flying in formation over Texas with a gander in lead or to observe a couple of angel fish swimming side by side under an oil well platform in the Persian Gulf with the male out front, or to observe a pack of wild dogs on the muddy beach in Iran with a male at the head of the pack, or to observe and Arab family in Egypt with the male and children walking eight paces ahead of the female, but it would be unusual to see a female leading these animals or fouls. Obviously nature had a specific place and duty for the male and female. On your approach to observe a gorilla family in South Africa, or when you step over a pasture fence in Georgia, the first confrontation would be with the male. If a law is enacted or a new legislature is formed, the first consideration is male obligation and his responsibility. In any sort of emergency the male is the first to respond regardless of his obligation.

During World War II wives of military men were allowed to lawfully divorce their husbands for desertion. This was done by the same law which approved and enforced the husband's absence. Some wives even chose to marry more than one serviceman which allowed her to receive more than one check from the government each month and if she could get those going into combat zones, she had a good chance of collecting several life insurance payoffs. After the war some of these laws were changed and the female began taking up her place in the family home once more. During the late 40's and early 50's there was a relatively domestic calm. The offspring received loving care and for the most part excellent guidance in home making and respect. Their school age achievements were greatly under the influence of their parents and their moral conduct was kept within the family's religious bonds. Recreation and sports were encouraged, which left little time for mischievous thoughts. Young ladies took interest in future homemakers and young men joined the future farmers. How little their parents knew, that in a few years homemakers would be home breakers and there would be no farms. You couldn't have convinced any parent at that time, dope and sex education were on the agenda just around the corner. You would have gotten no where explaining hippies, yippies, gays, equal rights, drugs, etc., to these people. The children of that era held their domestic relations together for the next twenty five years, but their offspring were short lived in married life. By early 1970, college campuses were rumbling with riots, drugs, sex, obscenities, vandalism and discontentment. No one seemed to know what they wanted in life, so they tried to make it hard for anyone to live decently. Students were only attending an average of two hours each day studies, so they had the time to pour it on. As a mature lieutenant said, "When I look back, I don't know how people could have stood me, when I was an ensign. I did such stupid things because I had authority and now, I feel so very ashamed." Whatever else these kids accomplished I never knew, but it did bring about a more rigid curriculum and many more working hours for them to accomplish their credits. At about the same time wives were pushing for equal rights, especially ex-wives and non-wives and homosexuals were coming out in force for them some rights on the streets. Majority groups were bellowing over all other voices and the government was hoping all this would go away. When it didn't they audited all the leaders back tax records and put most of them in jail, but some were left and their numbers multiplied. The government decided to compromise with a give and take program. They would give the under privileged woman a free schooling program known as Cedar (Center of Educational Development and Rehabilitation) and let the Mafia run it. They would give the students a heavier curriculum and if they didn't get back to work, the National Guard would force them. They would give the minority groups the right to burn down the town without any interference from the law. Also, for an added treat they could go to the same schools and churches while in the south, but this would be unconstitutional in the north. The news media, television and radio were living this up and kicking down big coins, this was the kind of hide and seek game they loved. They hired a man to hold morning talk shows on t.v. and radio with a live audience of housewives. He told them how to hide away portions of the husbands grocery money when shopping, how to put their money to use when they got a job (use it for make-up and buy some nice clothes, for carrying cash when they could sneak off to Austin's Palace Lounge for dancing with traveling men, and eventually buy their own car) and he encouraged them to get rid of the husbands while the children were underage. Also, he advised them to get all accounts made payable to Mr. or Mrs. instead of Mr. and Mrs., this way they could draw it all out before he got the message. Since they had minor children she could get the kids and he would have to pay a nice bundle of child support. Get a lawyer which could convince the judge of the need for permanent alimony, rather than a few years for rehabilitation. This would give her a life time meal ticket and sooner or later the government would enforce this pay, just as they had done the child support. He told them to get the checks sent through the courts so there wouldn't be any hassle on her part. Some schemes he talked of, were for the wife to get extra car keys made and hide them outside, pack her bags and deliver them to a friend's house ahead of time, have her boyfriend wait outside the house to occupy her husband while she made her get away. In short, when her husband came home from work, she would tell him things and get him angry, make him hit her one way or another, then run from the house screaming, so all the neighbors would be witnesses to the beating.

Another woman wanted to work at a lounge because she had class and was pretty and wanted to meet strange men. She said her husband made lots of money and would not consent to her exposure in a job of this sort. Her advise, was to secure the job while he was away working overseas, get all of her men friends set for him and just before he arrived, take out all the money and after his arrival her men friends would keep him run out of town until he became discouraged. Then she could divorce him for running off and leaving her.

Since I was working second shift, I had the opportunity to listen in, but I can imagine all the husbands which fell prey to this sort of tactics. Not once were any of them advised to discuss this with their husband.

Most men were becoming disgruntled about this time and knew something was coming down. They still had the responsibility of feeding and clothing the children, make house payments and pay all bills, so they really didn't have time to get involved. As a rule they gave their wives what she wanted and tried to keep her happy. A 71 year old man told me recently in Nashville, Tenn., that he and his wife had been happily married for 52 years. He said you're having trouble, Ken's wife left him and my other son's marriage isn't stable, but he said he never gave his wife what she wanted, he always gave her everything she needed.

In the late 70's, millions of housewives took to the industrial world and are steadily employed and with the employment situation in trouble, there hasn't been a single one of them back off and let the father of children work to feed the young. Most working women have a husband who is employed and even though their pay demands are equal, her wages aren't made available for use within the family. She works alongside a man of equal pay and when they arrive at the elevator, it torques her jaws if he gets on first and doesn't hold the door for her. The single and some married women want the man to open the car door, buy her dinner, drinks and pick up all the tabs, just to prove he's a fool. The divorced working woman has the advantage and best taste of all. She not only gets the equal wage and all the plush treatment from her men friends, but she has another check waiting in the mail each month. Sometimes it's her favorite boyfriend, which meets the postman, because he needs the check worse than she. Then there is the divorcee who lives in the plush apartment, lays by the pool all day and spends the nights dancing and entertaining men. This is all paid for by her previous husband, except the entertaining and she can always find a fool to foot that bill.

Some things these women don't know are statistics, these figures are creeping up behind them and when the axe falls, it will come down hard and sharp. Their age in time is moving very rapidly and by law, when the support ends, they won't be eligible for a single dime in any social security, retirement relief, medical, food or death benefit programs. These problems are going to engulf the developed and over-developed countries within the very near future and to most, it will be a rude awakening.

The divorce rate within countries condoning the women's equal rights movement have been and continues to skyrocket off the charts each month and men are becoming more and more aware of the uselessness of these women. In 1981 the government of Australia issued a discouraging publication to their men going abroad on meeting and marrying Far Eastern women however, that government admitted these marriages had been prosperous and only a very small percentage failed.

I've worked since I was seven years old and I've set many goals but after having these snatched from under me twice by American women and each time just as the end of the tunnel came into sight, I've begun to believe it's time to go east young man.

"RARE MIRACLE"

In summation the writer has progressed in many ways as life changed with the passing of time.

He attained a college level education during 21 years in the United States navy, ultimately retiring with 30 years of honorable service in 1980. During his naval career, he fathered two daughters and two sons by his first marriage. This marriage ended after 27 years and he lost his youngest son to a train accident in 1984. A second marriage failed after three years due to overseas employment and he married a lady from the Philippines in June 1984. As a result of the far eastern marriage, a new world record for child reproduction was established in July 1988 when the family was blessed with the arrival of a baby girl. The writer had been rendered totally sterile by vasectomy in December 1959 and this condition was reversed by microsurgery in February 1985. He had remained sterile for 25 years, 2 months and 2 days from time of vasectomy till time of reversal. After two years from reversal he became fertile for approximately three months, then returned to sterile making the arrival of the child in 1988 a "rare miracle" in reproduction. Currently the writer has a wife and young daughter, is happily married and works as a Senior Engineering Inspector for a prominent oil company in the offshore oil fields of the northern Arabic Gulf near Saudi Arabia.

1943 photo showing Thomas Kirk standing in front of his Uncle Leonard after his release from a German prison camp. Also shown in this photo - Aunt Margarett, Uncle Hoyt, Uncle Edwin, Aunt Rachel, Brother Kenneth, Sister Nora Jean and First Cousins Conrad and Carolyn Gay.

Grandfather David H. Kirk, Aunt Rachel and rabbit dogs, Luke and Queen.

Tom Kirk shown here with the children of the family. Uncle Horace, Uncle Hoyt, Uncle Edwin, Aunt Rachel, Brother Kenneth, Sister Nora Jean, First Cousins Conrad and Carolyn Gay, and Aunt Rhunett and Aunt Genevive.